THE REFERENCE SHELF (Contiued)

Volume 23

No.

2. Representative American Speeches: 1950-1951. A. C. Baird. $1.75.

No.

6. Gambling in America. H. L. Marx, Jr. $1.75.

Volume 22

No. 3. Representative American Speeches: 1949-1950. A. C. Baird. $1.75.

Volume 21

No. 2. Representative American Speeches: 1948-1949 A. C. Baird. $1.75.

Volume 20

No.

5. Federal World Government. J. E. Johnsen. $1.50.

No.

6. Federal Information Controls in Peacetime. R. E. Summers. $1.50.

Volume 19

No. 3. Free Medical Care. C. A. Peters. $1.25.

Volume 18

No.

3. Representative American Speeches: 1944-1945. A. C. Baird. $1.25.
5. Anatomy of Racial Intolerance. G. B. de Huszar. $1.25.

No.

6. Palestine: Jewish Homeland? J. E. Johnsen. $1.25.

Volume 17

No. 4. Representative American Speeches: 1943-1944. A. C. Baird. $1.25

Volume 16

No.

1. Representative American Speeches: 1941-1942. A. C. Baird. $1.25.

No.

6. Representative American Speeches: 1942-1943. A. C. Baird. $1.25.

THE REFERENCE SHELF

Vol. 28   No. 3

REPRESENTATIVE AMERICAN
SPEECHES: 1955-1956

Edited, and with Introductions
by
A. CRAIG BAIRD
Department of Speech, State University of Iowa

THE H. W. WILSON COMPANY
NEW YORK   1956

15707

PREFATORY NOTE

REPRESENTATIVE AMERICAN SPEECHES: 1955-56 is the nine-teenth in this annual series. Each volume contains some twenty "representative" speeches by Americans, or by others who have talked in this country (e.g., Winston Churchill and Anthony Eden). These nineteen volumes include about 400 addresses by some 280 speakers. (See Cumulative Author Index for full list of speakers and their speeches.)

These addresses have been grouped according to subject matter, such as International Policies, National Ideals, Agricul-ture, Business, Labor, Party Politics, Education, and Religion. Students of public address may prefer an alternate classification based upon the speakers' purposes, speaking occasions, speech types and audiences. The speeches in this volume would be classified somewhat as those before executive-administrative groups (Eisenhower, Gruenther), business and labor gatherings (Blakely, Hough, Richberg, Meany, Benson), dinner meetings (Hand, and others listed in this volume), college anniversaries (Aly), university baccalaureates (Dodds), educational confer-ences (de Kiewiet), political mass audiences (Eisenhower, Nixon, Stevenson), religious conferences (Scherer), sermons (O'Boyle, McCracken, Perilman), radio and television broadcasts (most of those speakers listed above).

This editor affirms in each volume that he makes no claim to selecting the "best" speeches of the year. He assumes that those addresses inserted have had more than passing significance —through the weight of ideas, or delivery, or through some combination of these speaking factors. He assumes that speech-making is to be estimated in terms of audience response, and that the large company of speakers in these nineteen volumes has influenced to some extent the social and other trends of the times.

The Introduction to each of the nineteen volumes deals with some phase of the problem and method of evaluating speeches and speechmakers. Successive volumes have treated such topics as the analysis and criticism of ideas, language, organization, and delivery. Some Introductions have summarized the important economic, political, social, and religious movements of the twelve-month period and the relation of the speeches to these events and trends. The present edition has attempted some comparison of political speaking of today and yesterday, this topic selected in view of the 1956 presidential campaign.

The brief introduction to each address gives the immediate setting and some reference to the speaker, occasion, and the speech itself. The student, it is assumed, will explore further the problems of textual authenticity, speaking occasion, thought, supporting details, structure, language, delivery, and the immediate and later effectiveness of the presentation.

The student is also referred to the biographical notes in the Appendix as the starting point in exploration of the speaker's background and those factors in his speech training and development related to his later methods and abilities on the platform.

The Table of Contents of each edition and the Cumulative Author Index at the end of this volume are further aids to a systematic review of speakers and issues since 1937. Here is found in epitome the sweep of recent American history as concretely reflected in the attitudes and conduct of speakers and the audience responses.

No one volume with its few speeches can well encompass a carefully balanced representation of the various political, educational, radio-television, religious, economic, and other spokesmen. The combined anthology of the four hundred examples, however, should provide a comprehensive cross-section of the various categories of speakers and speaking types.

This volume, like its predecessors, is a reference source, useful for subject information and for speakers and speeches to be studied as types. Each volume, in addition to its use as a library reference, is obviously of direct service to students of public speaking, extempore speaking, oral and written communication, discussion and debate, history and criticism of recent American public address, social science, and history, as well as to teachers of these subjects.

The editor is grateful to the various speakers and publishers for their cooperation in providing authentic texts and in giving permission for these reprints. Special acknowledgement is made in each case. This editor is also much indebted to the many students in his seminars who have investigated these contemporary speakers. He also appreciates the cooperation of the university libraries and their staffs—those, for example, at the University of Missouri, Florida State University, University of Mississippi, and especially Dr. Ralph Ellsworth, Director of Libraries, State University of Iowa, and his staff.

A. CRAIG BAIRD

March 1, 1956

CONTENTS

INTRODUCTION

POLITICAL SPEAKING TODAY AND YESTERDAY

How effective are the political speakers of the past twenty years as compared with those of our earlier public speaking history? Do our contemporary platform leaders, those prominent in statecraft, in state executive and legislative leadership, in Congress, in presidential, executive, or administrative positions, in political campaigning, measure up well compared with their counterparts of the late eighteenth, nineteenth, and the earlier twentieth century?

Who are the representative political speakers of the past twenty years? This investigator, during this score of years, along with his study of preachers, business and labor speakers, radio and television talkers, has reviewed these typical deliberative (that is, legislative-political) debaters and persuaders. As a basis for examination he has selected the following political talkers who have each appeared at least three times in the annual publications of REPRESENTATIVE AMERICAN SPEECHES since 1937: Dean G. Acheson, Alben W. Barkley, William E. Borah, Thomas E. Dewey, Paul H. Douglas, William O. Douglas, John Foster Dulles, Dwight D. Eisenhower, Herbert C. Hoover, David E. Lilienthal, Henry Cabot Lodge, Jr., Douglas MacArthur, Franklin D. Roosevelt, Adlai E. Stevenson, Robert A. Taft, Norman G. Thomas, Harry S. Truman, Arthur H. Vandenberg, Henry A. Wallace, and Wendell L. Willkie.[1]

These twenty are obviously not all of equal speaking ability. Doubtless the readers may prefer to eliminate some and to include others. Those listed above, nevertheless, will serve as illustrations of the significant political speakers of this period. Some are now dead; others were near the end of their active speaking twenty years ago; others have been prominent for a time but no longer have the public ear; still others are com-

[1] See Cumulative Author Index.

parative newcomers on the national scene and will presently comprise the bulk of the living American deliberative group.

What of their individual abilities and total impact in oral communication as compared with the effectiveness of Patrick Henry, Daniel Webster, Abraham Lincoln, and other orators of past centuries or more recent times? [2]

THEIR IDEAS

What of the inventive abilities of these deliberative speakers of 1936-1956? The weight of their ideas in their debates and other public addresses? According to popular impression platform speakers are to be gauged chiefly by their delivery. Critics of speechmakers, however, as Aristotle expounded in his *Rhetoric,* place thought or idea foremost in any judgment of effective oral discourse. The strength and originality of the ideas go far to determine the speaker's impress on his time and his rank among those of mature communicative excellence.

On a given occasion he may utter perfunctory thoughts. By and large, nevertheless, in his public career, he reveals on the platform distinctive traits of thinking and unusual intellectual penetration. He is a Webster who in his debates with Hayne sums up his country's history and outlines with vast wisdom the basis for its preservation. He is a Calhoun who, however mistaken he may be in the practical bearings of his nullification interpretation of our constitutional structure, nevertheless conceives with much insight robust postulates of government. He is a Douglas and a Lincoln battling in Illinois in 1858 to clarify for all time the issues on the settlement of which our national destiny depends.

What are these traits of intellect? The effective political speaker has mental range and consistency of principles. In the light of such premises and assumptions he measures the economic, political, social problems of his day. Furthermore he has ability to analyze a topic, to detect and frame the fundamental questions at stake. On such basis he summons his evidence and makes his inferences.

[2] A. Craig Baird, *American Public Addresses: 1740-1952* (McGraw-Hill, 1956)

In addition to this breadth of thinking and this ability to analyze, the superior political speaker as thinker is an economic-social-political philosopher. Not content to present merely the expedient and the obvious, he views the problem in its larger context. He is a historian and logician. He generalizes, traces causes and results, and relates the specific problem to its larger relationships. He is thus a genuine philosopher as was Burke. But he is also a practical down-to-earth politician. His speculations are of the living and demanding world. But he approaches statesmanship as he counsels and persuades. For he is thinker as well as compiler and word manipulator.

What can be said of the thinking of our contemporaries in their legislative and executive eloquence? In this philosophical grasp of contemporary perplexities are they chiefly deficient. Because they lack educational discipline, or because they are preoccupied with material concerns, or because they yield completely to the mass mind and attitudes, most of them are limited in their philosophic imagination.

Most senators and House members, for example, move almost entirely among economic and other details. Many of these debaters and discussants are apparently unconscious of the broader currents on which their minutiae sweep along. Some owe their Senate seats to vote-getting popularity and to traits other than mental acuity. The better Senate debaters are well armed with statistics and communicate out of legal formulas which most of them have assimilated. But few of them are James Madisons capable of handling with authority and wisdom the issues of centralized government, taxation, constitutional changes. Their definitions, analyses, and argumentative developments are usually circumscribed. They are school and college debaters grown older. Here and there a speaker rises in the Senate with breadth and statesmanship as he discusses the tariff or recognition of Red China. Paul Douglas, of Illinois, for example, though he moves through reams of statistics, occasionally flashes out with passages that illuminate the wider horizon.[3]

[3] See Paul Douglas, "Foreign Policy," *Representative American Speeches: 1950-51*, p72-4.

What can be said of the invention (thought, ideas) of the political stump speakers in recent campaigns? Perhaps we should draw the curtain on speaking activities in the campaigns of 1952, 1954, and 1956. The jargon of the heated appeals must give pause to those who search for intellectual balance and genuine acumen. Much of this political violence, we agree, characterized the older days. But have we made progress?

Why this mediocrity in Congress, in much executive and administrative speaking, and on the stump?

As I suggested above, too often the speaker has pitched his discourse to the lower popular mind and spirit. As Timothy Sheehan, representative to Congress from Illinois, has been quoted: "I'm no statesman. I vote the way the people want me to unless they're absolutely wrong." Hence the glittering generalities, the name calling, the bandwagon appeals—and the other practices of bad propaganda.

The real weakness, perhaps inevitable in our expanding democracy, lies in the general lack of training in public affairs and the accompanying training in oral communication. In this day of more and more complex problems, it would seem that our political spokesmen should be especially well grounded in history, economics, government, logic, philosophy, as well as in literature and science. These deficiencies in training—training obtained either in schools or through prolonged independent study—are obvious. By contrast the foremost political speakers —those that impress their countrymen through the years and find their places in speech anthologies—have had such competency. Franklin D. Roosevelt, at Groton and Harvard, Woodrow Wilson at Princeton, John Hopkins, and elsewhere, had such development. (These examples do not imply that all statesmen-speakers must attend these or any other universities.) But if governmental and rear platform speakers of this hour are to command our attention and respect through their vigor of thought, a broad educational background, however derived, is essential.

ORAL LANGUAGE

A second test of political speaking lies in language efficiency. The superior political persuader is at home with word meanings. He has absorbed much of the richness of our vocabulary. He achieves accuracy of statement, clarity in his adaptation to all kinds of listeners, and connotative liveliness. His style is oral and individual—it is never that of some classroom or even of some ghost writer. For his words reflect his own personality. His texture of expression is fresh and distinctive. According to the occasion he is naturally eloquent or stylistically factual, and restrained.

What of the political speeches of our day with respect to language? Commonplaceness, mediocrity, triteness are too often unrelieved. Neither the speaker nor his ghost writer has imagination or emotion—or consciousness that language is the link between effective thinking and full audience response.

Another group of speakers resorts to language of the other extreme—of embellishment and decoration. Albert J. Beveridge (before 1902) and others of his generation were guilty of this floridity—with extreme figures of speech, extended parallelisms, and general exaggeration of statement. Occasional speakers of our time have echoed this earlier exuberance. Senator William E. Borah sometimes became overly oratorical. (I refer here solely to language, and not to delivery.) General Douglas MacArthur, a superior speaker, has also sometimes indulged in excesses of language, though on the whole his eloquence is of the man and commands high rating.[4] Franklin D. Roosevelt, even after we discount his able speech writers, occasionally attained superiority in his compositional originality. So did Dwight D. Eisenhower, in his inaugural address, rise above stylistic mediocrity. Adlai E. Stevenson, however, among recent political communicators, has delivered speech after speech couched in urbane, dignified phrases unmatched since the platform originality of Woodrow Wilson.[5]

[4] See Douglas MacArthur, "Seventy-fifth Birthday Address," *Representative American Speeches: 1954-55*, p34-42.

[5] See Cumulative Author Index for references to speeches by Franklin D. Roosevelt, Dwight D. Eisenhower, and Adlai E. Stevenson.

Delivery

A third test of the contemporary political speaker is his delivery. How does he compare with Patrick Henry, Webster, Ingersoll, Bryan in vocal ability? The superior speaker has desirable vocal pitch; effective vocal intensity or loudness (with proper use of pauses); desirable rate; and excellent voice quality. He projects to his audience. And his articulation and pronunciation are acceptable. He has impressive physical bearing and uses meaningful gestures. He is usually fluent, skilled in extemporizing. If he refers to his manuscript, he does so with constant alertness to his listeners.

Unfortunately few excel in all of these categories. We therefore describe the speaker as high or low in the composite rating of his vocal and physical abilities.

The best of our recent political speakers have their limitations in delivery. Franklin D. Roosevelt was easy and conversational—at the top in his radio communication. But his rate (sometimes as slow as 110 words per minute) and his pitch were adversely criticized.[6]   Harry Truman's delivery in his speech of March 12, 1947, was marked by a "flat, undramatic reading, with a Middle Western accent and in a monotone."[7] William E. Borah in his Senate speech on October 2, 1939, "was scarcely audible when he began."[8]   Herbert Hoover, in 1940, was judged as having a voice "with a degree of monotone; his control of vowels and consonants is not always effective in radio addresses; he occasionally lapses into measured reading habits."[9]   John Foster Dulles "is no orator."[10]   President Eisenhower "makes no pretense at oratory, and often develops a monotony of vocal pattern as he reads. But his voice and visible manner continue to convey sincerity and have been important in helping him to retain strong popularity."[11]

[6] *Representative American Speeches: 1939-40*, p21-2.
[7] *Representative American Speeches: 1946-47*, p43.
[8] *Representative American Speeches: 1939-40*, p43.
[9] *Representative American Speeches: 1939-40*, p 128.
[10] *Representative American Speeches: 1954-55*, p 19.
[11] *Representative American Speeches: 1954-55*, p71.

Senator Robert Taft, in his Senate speech of January 5 in 1951, "followed closely his manuscript and often spoke with accelerated, rather high pitched, impatient, but not irascible tones. He was nevertheless superior in his extempore readiness." [12] Senator Paul Douglas was sometimes affected by vocal tightness. In his Senate speech of January 15, 1951, he "read his address, but accepted many interruptions and injected extempore replies that demonstrate his versatility in extempore speaking." [13] Thomas Dewey, although diagnosed as over-precise in his articulation, in his acceptance speech at Chicago, June 28, 1944, "impressed more by his voice and personality than by his subject matter. He was smiling, self-assured, at ease with his manuscript and his audience. His voice had wide range, flexibility, pleasant modulation and excellent quality. . . ." [14] These speakers and others listed at the outset of this article all had weaknesses in some aspects of delivery. But whatever their vocal limitations they all are to be rated as high in general delivery. Why? All had at least one characteristic that set them off from mediocre talkers: they were all communicative. However they managed their voices, waved their arms or violated other principles of correct bodily control, they knew how to project to their audiences, hold attention, and in the end—in the Senate, over the air, or at whistle stops—evoke spontaneous and repeated response.

Are the speakers of the past twenty years inferior in delivery to the best of former times? We doubt it. The development of cinema, radio and television, the trends in popular education toward extempore speaking, the rise of speech departments, and the increased practice of speaking in adult education and in industrial and professional speaking activity, have all encouraged improved vocal habits. Our present political speakers no doubt lack the formal eloquence of the late eighteenth and the nineteenth century, but on the whole have facility with audiences that well matches the skills of the older orators.

[12] *Representative American Speeches: 1950-51,* p65.
[13] *Representative American Speeches: 1950-51,* p72.
[14] *Representative American Speeches: 1943-44,* p260.

THE SPEAKER'S PERSONALITY AND CHARACTER

One other test of effective political speaking has to do with the speaker's personality or character. Certainly personality—the total physical, mental, and emotional resources—as reflected in the communicative process—strongly affects what happens in the speech. Ralph Waldo Emerson's definition of eloquence has been often quoted: "the art of speaking what you mean and are." [15]

Three important traits of character, Aristotle affirms in *Rhetoric,* we expect our speakers to reveal: (1) their intellectual integrity (honesty); (2) their good will (social adaptiveness and proper respect for and faith in their audiences; and (3) moral force and courage.

These elements are in the long run reflected in the speaker's ideas, language, audience adaptation, and delivery. We have more faith in him—respond favorably to him—if he has common honesty, sincerity, tact, high ethical and religious principles.

Do our contemporary speakers rank well in these qualities as compared with Calhoun, Clay, Webster, Douglas, Lincoln, and the others of our speaking tradition?

We continue to have politicians whose tongues are free, whose words are facile, and yet whose motives and appeals are inimical to the welfare of our individual and collective citizens. The demagogues continue to have their day—with their ignorance, prejudices, lies, and chicanery—and with their many followers. Walter Lippmann observes:

> With exceptions so rare they are regarded as miracles of nature, successful democratic politicians are insecure and intimidated men. They advance politically only as they placate, appease, bribe, seduce, bamboozle, or otherwise manage to manipulate the demanding, threatening elements in their constituencies. The decisive consideration is not whether the proposition is good but whether it is popular—not whether it will work well and prove itself, but whether the active-talking constituents like it immediately.[16]

Have present-day speakers, then, deteriorated in moral courage in their public utterances? I do not think so. Neither does

[15] Lester Thonssen and A. Craig Baird, *Speech Criticism* (Ronald Press, 1948), "The Character of the Speaker," p383.
[16] Walter Lippmann, *The Public Philosophy* (Little, Brown, 1955), p27.

Senator John Kennedy, of Massachusetts. Says the senator: "I am convinced that the complication of public business and the competition for the public's attention have obscured innumerable acts of political courage—large and small—performed almost daily in the Senate Chamber." [17]

Thus President Eisenhower, as cited above, has steadily convinced millions of his intellectual and moral integrity. Robert A. Taft likewise displayed from start to finish moral independence and courage that gave him high respect as a political debater.

So are similar traits evident in Herbert Hoover, Henry Cabot Lodge, Adlai E. Stevenson, Norman Thomas, and the others we have listed. And why are certain headline senatorial and other political speakers not included? Because we the public have withheld our judgment and confidence concerning their intellectual and moral attitudes and motives.

Have those of the past score of years shown less conscience and moral stability than their political forebears? Daniel Webster in his Seventh of March, 1850, Address supporting compromise measures on slavery brought down upon himself the indignation of almost all of New England and sank into obloquy. But his like in courage, as Senator Kennedy affirms, can be duplicated by present day statesmen-speakers—though perhaps not under such dramatic conditions as those of 1850. The trend of moral courage, despite the many exceptions, is by no means downward.

* * *

In conclusion, what political speakers of this mid-century will survive, to be analyzed by students fifty years hence? Public address is primarily for the moment. Its immediate effect is to be gauged by the resulting votes or other tangible evidence. The competition for survival in public speech, like that in literature, art, drama, and other realms of creativity, will doom to early oblivion most of those we now exalt. Those who are now included in the yearly anthologies and who have their discourses printed in full in the New York *Times* and elsewhere

[17] John Kennedy, "Challenge of Political Courage," New York *Times Magazine*, p 13, December 8, 1955.

will be replaced by others whose day stars are rising. These in turn another generation will eclipse. Only one or two of each period, those who affect American history and thought, will live. We assume and believe, nevertheless, that each generation of public orators will have fulfilled the best traditions of effective public address and will continue to express "the best aspirations of the people in dignified honest speech." [18] Thus will American civilization continue to be motivated toward a genuinely good and enduring society.

[18] Thonssen and Baird, *Speech Criticism* p472.

INTERNATIONAL RELATIONS

FIRST STEPS IN DISARMAMENT [1]

Dwight D. Eisenhower [2]

President Dwight D. Eisenhower gave this address on Thursday, July 21, 1955, at a session of the Big Four Conference at Geneva, Switzerland. President Eisenhower proposed that the United States and Russia have mutual inspection by continuous aerial reconnaissance of each other's complete military establishments. The assumption was that with such complete blueprinted and visually observed information about the atomic and hydrogen military production, the exposure of any preparations for surprise atomic attacks would be assured. Thus a practical move toward disarmament would be initiated.

The entire conference lasted from Monday, July 18, through Saturday of that week. President Eisenhower, chairman at the opening session, reminded his three colleagues of their object: "to generate and put in motion the new forces to set us truly on the path to peace." He listed the West's chief topics for discussion: German unification, European security, removing the "iron curtain," and disarmament. The others of the Big Four, Bulganin of Russia, Edgar Faure of France, Sir Anthony Eden of Great Britain, each presented an approach to these problems.

The Russians quickly made it plain that they would not approve of any German unification until NATO was abolished and replaced by an all-European system of collective security.

For four days the conversations continued with obvious deadlock and without any hope of any concerted program. President Eisenhower constantly injected into the deliberations a note of optimism and friendly cooperation. For example, he and General Zhukov renewed their old-time military comradeship.

On Thursday afternoon came Eisenhower's dramatic and concrete proposal. (The French and British prime ministers had received no previous information about the President's suggestion; and few, if any, American leaders outside the State Department had been briefed concerning the plan.) Eisenhower began by reading his formal statement, "but midway removed his glasses and looking at the Russians, spoke extemporaneously" (*Time*, 66:20, August 1, 1955). His specific proposal for mutual inspection of military establishments and movements as a "beginning," and his

---

[1] Text with permission for this reprint furnished through the courtesy of Mr. James Hagerty, press secretary of President Dwight D. Eisenhower.

[2] For biographical note, see Appendix.

concrete program for disarmament and the lessening of military and political tensions caught the Russians and the other delegates by surprise.
The Russians at the moment had no answer. Premier Faure immediately
spoke up:

> I wish the peoples of the world could have been in this
> conference room to hear the voice of a man speaking from great
> military experience. Had this been possible, they would believe
> that something had changed in the world in the handling of
> this question of disarmament. I am sure that this conference has
> scored its first victory over skepticism.

Sir Anthony Eden praised Eisenhower's "eloquent proposal" and
was "deeply moved by the sincerity and warm feeling for peace."

The final meetings were given to a framing of a communiqué.
With no questions resolved, but with a climate of cordiality established,
it was agreed that a meeting of the Big Four ministers should be held
at Geneva in October to grapple more directly with these problems.
Back in Moscow Premier Bulganin gave a generally temperate report on
Geneva, but implied rejection by the USSR of the Eisenhower proposal
for mutual inspection of military establishments.

For three weeks, beginning during the last week of October and
ending on November 16, 1955, the foreign ministers of the Big Four
(John Foster Dulles, United States; V. M. Molotov, Russia; Antoine
Pinay, France; Harold MacMillan, Great Britain) also talked at Geneva.
From the outset it was apparent that no meeting of diplomatic minds was
possible. Toward the end the "Geneva spirit" had fallen to a low estate.
As Secretary of State Dulles put it: "I wonder whether an agreement with
the Soviet Union is worth much." And Foreign Minister Molotov replied,
"The positions of the three [Western] powers are not of a constructive
nature." The Russians took a blunt and bleak position against a united
Germany in NATO. They proposed an All-German Council that would
obviously result in the eventual communization of that nation.

In the deliberations the West argued for President Eisenhower's
plan of mutual inspection. Russia insisted that such a proposal should
be considered only as part of a general disarmament program—obviously
a vague and indeterminate line of discussion that would sidestep for
several years any specific solution of the problem of surprise attack by
Russia. For lessening the barriers to East-West free communication,
Russia apparently would support only a program of cultural exchange—
and only at an official level.

Thus the spirit and hopes of Geneva I were completely dashed at
Geneva II. The cold war was apparently to revive. Events of the subse-
quent months, for example, Russia's political, economic, and military
drives in the Middle and Far East, marked this sinister trend.

Mr. Chairman, Gentlemen:

Disarmament is one of the most important subjects on our agenda. It is also extremely difficult. In recent years the scientists have discovered methods of making weapons many, many times more destructive of opposing armed forces—but also of homes, and industries and lives—than ever known or even imagined before. These same scientific discoveries have made much more complex the problems of limitation and control and reduction of armament.

After our victory as Allies in World War II, my country rapidly disarmed. Within a few years our armament was at a very low level. Then events occurred beyond our borders which caused us to realize that we had disarmed too much. For our own security and to safeguard peace we needed greater strength. Therefore we proceeded to rearm and to associate with others in a partnership for peace and for mutual security.

The American people are determined to maintain and if necessary increase this armed strength for as long a period as is necessary to safeguard peace and to maintain our security.

But we know that a mutually dependable system for less armament on the part of all nations would be a better way to safeguard peace and to maintain our security.

It would ease the fears of war in the anxious hearts of people everywhere. It would lighten the burdens upon the backs of the people. It would make it possible for every nation, great and small, developed and less developed, to advance the standards of living of its people, to attain better food, and clothing, and shelter, more of education and larger enjoyment of life.

Therefore the United States Government is prepared to enter into a sound and reliable agreement making possible the reduction of armament. I have directed that an intensive and thorough study of this subject be made within our own government. From these studies, which are continuing, a very important principle is emerging to which I referred in my opening statement on Monday.

No sound and reliable agreement can be made unless it is completely covered by an inspection and reporting system adequate to support every portion of the agreement.

The lessons of history teach us that disarmament agreements without adequate reciprocal inspection increase the dangers of war and do not brighten the prospects of peace.

Thus it is my view that the priority attention of our combined study of disarmament should be upon the subject of inspection and reporting.

Questions suggest themselves.

How effective an inspection system can be designed which would be mutually and reciprocally acceptable within our countries and the other nations of the world? How would such a system operate? What could it accomplish?

Is certainty against surprise aggression attainable by inspection? Could violations be discovered promptly and effectively counteracted?

We have not as yet been able to discover any scientific or other inspection method which would make certain of the elimination of nuclear weapons. So far as we are aware no other nation has made such a discovery. Our study of this problem is continuing. We have not as yet been able to discover any accounting or other inspection method of being certain of the true budgetary facts of total expenditures for armament. Our study of this problem is continuing. We by no means exclude the possibility of finding useful checks in these fields.

As you can see from these statements, it is our impression that many past proposals of disarmament are more sweeping than can be insured by effective inspection.

Gentlemen, since I have been working on this memorandum to present to this conference, I have been searching my heart and mind for something that I could say here that could convince everyone of the great sincerity of the United States in approaching this problem of disarmament.

I should address myself for a moment principally to the delegates from the Soviet Union, because our two great countries admittedly possess new and terrible weapons in quantities which do give rise in other parts of the world, or reciprocally, to the fears and dangers of surprise attack.

I propose, therefore, that we take a practical step, that we begin an arrangement, very quickly, as between ourselves— immediately. These steps would include:

To give to each other a complete blueprint of our military establishments, from beginning to end, from one end of our countries to the other; lay out the establishments and provide the blue prints to each other.

Next, to provide within our countries facilities for aerial photography to the other country—we to provide you the facilities within our country, ample facilities for aerial reconnaissance, where you can make all the pictures you choose and take them to your own country to study, you to provide exactly the same facilities for us and we to make these examinations, and by this step to convince the world that we are providing as between ourselves against the possibility of great surprise attack, thus lessening danger and relaxing tension. Likewise we will make more easily attainable a comprehensive and effective system of inspection and disarmament, because what I propose, I assure you, would be but a beginning.

Now from my statements I believe you will anticipate my suggestion. It is that we instruct our representatives in the subcommittee on disarmament in discharge of their mandate from the United Nations to give priority effort to the study of inspection and reporting. Such a study could well include a step by step testing of inspection and reporting methods.

The United States is ready to proceed in the study and testing of a reliable system of inspections and reporting, and when that system is proved, then to reduce armaments with all others to the extent that the system will provide assured results.

The successful working out of such a system would do much to develop the mutual confidence which will open wide the avenues of progress for all our peoples.

The quest for peace is the statesman's most exacting duty. Security of the nation entrusted to his care is his greatest responsibility. Practical progress to lasting peace is his fondest hope. Yet in pursuit of his hope he must not betray the trust placed in him as guardian of the people's security. A sound peace—with security, justice, well-being, and freedom for the people of the world—can be achieved, but only by patiently and thoughtfully following a hard and sure and tested road.

THE NORTH ATLANTIC TREATY ORGANIZATION AND DEFENSE OF WESTERN EUROPE [3]

ALFRED M. GRUENTHER [4]

General Alfred M. Gruenther, Supreme Allied Commander in Europe, military commander of the North Atlantic Treaty Organization, gave this address before the Italian Center for the Study of International Reconciliation, Banco di Roma, Italy, on May 2, 1955.

His Rome audience, typical of many that Gruenther addressed in Europe since his appointment as Supreme Commander in July 1953, included the ambassadors and plenipotentiary ministers of fifteen countries of the Atlantic Pact, numerous representatives of many other countries of Europe, Asia, and Africa, numerous Italian diplomats, the highest military and civilian authorities, as well as other important political, economic, cultural, and journalistic representatives in Rome.

General Gruenther here followed his usual pattern of speech ideas and organization. He presented clearly his central theme—(1) today the free world is threatened by the Soviet Union and her satellites, and (2) NATO is our dependable defense. His speaking aim was to "sell" his program. His introduction was relatively long—to gain rapport with his somewhat skeptical audience.

To support his thesis he reasoned logically and factually with emotional appeals, to fear (of Russian aggression), to the spirit of Western unity, to love of religion, and to his personal prestige. He skillfully established his own good will, character, and sagacity.[5]

His language here, as in his other speeches, was concise, terse, easily comprehended, with a sprinkling of anecdotes and stories.

The General's unusual memory aids his delivery. Whether or not he refers to a manuscript, he is extempore, informal, brisk. His personality is friendly, humorous. His voice is easy to listen to, "crisp, metallic, sharp, but very pleasant, each word carefully enunciated, yet artfully preserving a Nebraska accent." [6]

[3] Text supplied through the courtesy of Lieutenant Colonel H. Glen Wood, special assistant to the Supreme Allied Commander in Europe, with permission of General Alfred M. Gruenther, Supreme Allied Commander in Europe, for this reprint.

[4] For biographical note, see Appendix.

[5] Donald Dedmon, "Rhetorical Analysis of Four Representative Speeches of General Alfred M. Gruenther on the North Atlantic Treaty Organization," graduate thesis at the State University of Iowa, January 1956.

[6] T. H. White, New York *Times Magazine*, p 12, July 12, 1953.

General Gruenther announced his forthcoming retirement from the military command of the North Atlantic Treaty Organization, and from the United States Army, in April 1956.

Eccellenze, Signore e Signori:

It is a great honor for me to be here this evening. I wish I could speak to you in Italian—in perfect Italian—with, of course, a slight Nebraska accent. But that would be a bit difficult for me. I beg of you to excuse me if I now proceed in English—also with a Nebraska accent.

I feel that it is a sad commentary on the state of the world that you should find it appropriate to have a military man talk to this distinguished group in the year 1955. Unfortunately, however, the question of security is our main preoccupation in this uneasy world.

I came to Italy for the first time in 1919 after we had just finished one world war. In fact I played a major role in ending that war. I was a cadet at the United States Military Academy, scheduled to be graduated in 1921. The state of the war got to be so crucial that the United States Government decided to graduate our class early, specifically on the first of November 1918. The Kaiser heard about this significant increase in Allied strength and eleven days later he surrendered. However, the United States Government now had 278 new second lieutenants on its hands, and there was little use for them. The decision was made to send us to Europe on a tour of observation and study. We visited Italy in the summer of 1919 absolutely convinced then that our profession would never be needed again in the new and better world which was just getting under way.

The next time I came to Italy was in September 1943, when there was a very great need for the military. We landed at Salerno as a part of General Clark's allied force, and in the eighteen months that followed I learned about war. My course of instruction lasted from the ninth of September 1943 until July 1945. By that time we had moved up the Italian peninsula to Verona.   If I did not know of the futility of war earlier, I certainly had it impressed upon me indelibly during my experiences in Italy.   I want to say, at the same time, that we learned to respect the Italian people.   The assistance we received from the Italian Resistance movement made a very significant contribution to the success of the Allied Italian campaign. I want to thank the people from Italy now for the magnificent assistance you gave us.

Then came VE-Day on May 8, 1945.   From Verona, I moved on to Vienna where I joined our allies, the Soviets; I saw much of them for the next several months.   In Vienna we concerned ourselves with the problems of occupation.   I was confident that we had reached a good understanding and that international tension was a thing of the past.   But in September 1945 those tensions began to reappear, and we experienced a chill in the Soviet climate.

Nevertheless, the Western Allies continued to demobilize, but the Soviets did not.   Soon a series of frictions developed, culminating in such incidents as the Czechoslovakian coup and the Berlin blockade.   As a result, a number of the former Allies found that they had to build a collective security organization in order to preserve the peace.   It was called the North Atlantic Treaty Organization, and that treaty was signed on April 4, 1949.

But NATO didn't make much progress until the free world was once again shocked by the advent of war—this time the invasion of South Korea in June 1950.   That act of aggression made it crystal clear that rapid progress was needed in perfecting our defense organization.

General Eisenhower arrived in Europe in January 1951 to organize the defense of Europe from the northern tip of Norway to the eastern borders of Turkey—a distance of seven thousand kilometers.   He came as the servant of the North Atlantic Treaty Organization—twelve nations then, now fourteen.   I was General Eisenhower's Chief of Staff.   He arrived in Paris on the seventh of January 1951.   After a three day survey in

Paris he started his trips; first to Brussels, then The Hague, then to Denmark, Norway, England, Portugal, and Italy. We arrived in Rome on the eighteenth of January 1951.

I would like to tell you what the situation was then. First of all, the morale of the free world was at a very low ebb. We had practically no strength. When General Eisenhower returned to Paris from this trip on the twenty-fourth of January 1951, he had a meeting of his commanders. I can remember the conference very well, because there was present one very sour-looking officer, a general, who seemed to be rather unhappy about the state of the world. General Eisenhower asked the question: "What do you think the Soviets would need to move to the English Channel?" This despondent general said, "General, they need only one thing—boots!" This was his cynical way of saying that we had no defense worthy of the name.

It is now four years and a few months since that conference took place. I can tell you that since that time our forces throughout our area have increased from three to four times numerically from what they were then, and when one considers the question of effectiveness, the increase is greater still. I can assure you that nobody can march to the Channel now by just putting his boots on. It would require more men and more air support to move the men in those boots. Most important of all, the free world has become convinced that the only answer to this problem is collective security. If we had had a NATO organization in 1939, even with the defects that ours has now—and I can assure you it still has many—I'm convinced there would have been no World War II. If we could have served notice at that time that an attack on one nation would be considered as an attack on all, Hitler would have been dissuaded from attacking.

In any case that is what the free nations have decided on; that is the goal toward which they are building. They are now absolutely dedicated to the idea that no nation—be it large or small—is sufficient unto itself in this jet-atomic age. That is our doctrine, and therein lies our greatest progress and our greatest strength.

We now have a going concern. We have an over-all head-quarters at SHAPE [Supreme Headquarters, Allied Powers in Europe] in Paris, and four subordinate headquarters. We have a northern command at Oslo that has for its mission the defense of Norway and Denmark; a headquarters at Fontainebleau for the defense of the critical central area; a headquarters at Naples for the defense of Italy, Greece and Turkey; and a headquarters at Malta for the protection of the vital Mediterranean sea-lines of communication.

Those headquarters study the problems of not what a possible enemy may decide to do, but what he *could* do. We refer to that capacity in military jargon as "capabilities." We do not try to assess enemy intentions; that would be very dangerous. This is what we find: That the Soviet bloc now constitutes some eight hundred million people—the most powerful empire in the history of the world. From the standpoint of military strength, it has in the Soviet Union itself approximately 175 infantry divisions comprising 2.5 million men. From the standpoint of air power, it has some twenty thousand Soviet operational aircraft. From the standpoint of naval power it has a relatively weak surface navy, but a strong submarine fleet. To give you just an idea of Soviet naval power, I can cite that the Soviet Navy now has approximately 350 submarines of all classes, big and little, good and bad. To get an idea of what 350 submarines mean, please bear in mind that when World War II began, the Germans had approximately seventy-five submarines. That does not mean that the Soviets are five times as good as the Germans were then, because the Soviets do not have the "know-how"; but it is an indication of where they are placing their emphasis.

In addition to the Soviet forces, there are between seventy-five and eighty satellite divisions, not nearly as good as the Soviet ones; but the Soviets know that and they are doing their best to improve them. The satellites have between two and three thousand aircraft, again not nearly as good as the Soviets' but they are improving. The satellite navies are relatively small and ineffective.

Those are the forces of the Soviet bloc. They are the forces which we at SHAPE use as the basis for our planning. We notice that the Soviet armed forces are constantly increasing in effectiveness. We do not say that these forces are ever going to be used. To speculate in that field is not our job. Our task is to plan to make an act of aggression by those forces so expensive that it will never take place. In other words, our prime objective is to prevent a third world war.

Yesterday was May Day in Moscow. May Day has traditionally been a celebration for the workers. However, in Moscow for the last several years, it has turned into an armed forces demonstration. Last year the Soviets showed some new airplanes; it was expected they would show some new planes yesterday. But it rained very, very heavily and so no new planes appeared. I think it is well, however, for us to bear in mind that if we had had one of these Italian sunshiny days yesterday, you would have had big headlines today concerning new types of airplanes the Soviets had perfected within the last year. I mention that not to create any fear in your hearts, but merely to bring to your attention some of the grim realities that we're facing.

We at SHAPE have been given the problem of planning for the defense of Europe. Our mission is twofold: to defend our European territory—all of it; and secondly, in the event of an all-out act of aggression, to defeat the enemy. Notice that I do not say to "win," because I'm convinced that if there should be a third world war there would be no winner. However, it is essential that we be able to defeat an enemy.

The next question is how well could we do now? Are we good enough to defend this seven-thousand-kilometer perimeter against an all-out attack now? Considering where we were four years ago, it would be nothing short of a miracle if we had developed that much strength in such a short period of time. Our forces were at a pitifully low level in 1951. In the year before General Eisenhower came over here—1950—the budget of the European nations for defense was approximately five billion dollars. Last year—1954—the budget in those same countries had gone up to $13.5 billion. However, it takes time

to implement defense measures, and so we're not yet strong
enough to be certain of resisting successfully an all-out attack.
Therefore, with respect to the first mission I have described—
to defend our European territory—we cannot give that assurance
yet. It was for that reason that when General Eisenhower was
the supreme commander, he recommended a German contribution.

A week from today in Paris, Signor Martino will be present
at the meeting of the Foreign Ministers in Paris when Germany
is admitted to NATO. As your chairman has stated, Germany
will become the fifteenth member of NATO. We will then
get, in due course, a German military contribution. That contribution will consist of some thirteen hundred tactical aircraft,
twelve army divisions; and some naval craft, for use generally
in the Baltic area. When the German forces are effective,
which will be in three to four years from now, we will be able
to defend Europe even against an all-out act of aggression.
That is the military reason why we have constantly advocated
this German contribution.

The admission of Germany to NATO, however, has more
than military significance. It is the beginning of a new Europe.
We all have high hopes for the Europe which is going to
evolve from this arrangement. I think the Italians should feel
particularly proud of the role that Italy has played to bring it
about. Certainly, Prime Minister Alcide de Gasperi was one
of the small group that sponsored the idea initially. It was he
who spoke to General Eisenhower—he and Count Sforza—in
January 1951, when General Eisenhower came here to Rome.
Both of these distinguished Italians had long shared the concept of a united Europe. I'm sorry they cannot be present at
the Palais de Chaillot a week from today.

I have said that we cannot be sure of accomplishing our first
mission—that is, the defense of Europe—now, but that when we
get the German contribution we shall be. Because I have said
it will take three or four years before that German contribution
is effective, you may have in mind the question: "Doesn't that
mean that we are in mortal peril during those three to four
years?" Although there is no exact answer to that question,

I'd like to make an observation on it. At this time—the second of May 1955—our side has a tremendous advantage over the Soviet bloc in the field of long-range airpower. A little over a year ago an American plane, the B-47, of which there are many in the American Air Force, flew from Maine over to England in four hours and thirty-four minutes. That is an average speed of about eleven hundred kilometers an hour.

At this stage of technological development, there is no answer to that plane. The Soviets do not have an answer to that plane, and we do not have an answer either. We have a significant number of those planes. For that reason, if a war should break out today, and if my most pessimistic assumption should prove correct—that the aggressor should overrun Europe —he would still be defeated because he does not have an answer to these long-range airplanes. Even if it had been a sunshiny day in Moscow yesterday, the answer would not have been shown. . . . There might have been new planes displayed, and I'm sure there would have been. But it will take some time before the Soviets can get them to Detroit, Pittsburgh and Chicago, which they must be able to do before they can defeat us. I do not want to say that the time is not coming when they can do that, but what I do want to say is that the time has not yet arrived when they can surpass us in long-range air power. Moreover, if we are vigilant that day will never arrive. In other words I do not feel that the situation is at all hopeless. We must maintain our courage. I don't want to appear complacent about this matter, but at the same time I don't want to be hysterical either.

I know that in a group of this kind it is unnecessary to say that security consists of more—much more—than just the military strength. It consists of economic and psychological elements as well. The economic element speaks for itself. However, I'd like to devote a few moments to the psychological aspects.

We have made tremendous progress in this alliance of ours —much greater success than we ever thought possible four years ago. We are much farther along than the estimates which we made in April 1951. That does not mean, however, that the path for the future is going to be a smooth one. My belief is that the next four years are going to be harder than the last four years, and largely because of the difficulty in solving the psychological problems.

We will have the problem of creating a public opinion stout-hearted enough to continue through this cold war no matter how long it lasts, and it may last a long, long time. Our people are peace-loving, and it is very difficult for them to keep up their enthusiasm for defense burdens that are so heavy —and may grow even heavier. There is also a very strong peace offensive being waged now by the Communists. In this campaign the Communists are attempting by neutralist propaganda to divide and split our alliance. The Soviets are very clever in this propaganda business.

When I left Italy in the summer of 1945, I went to Vienna, and there for the next four months I saw a great deal of the Soviets. There I met one of the ablest officers I have ever known in any service. He was a Russian, aged forty-two, a four-star general. He was the number two man under Marshal Koniev who, as you saw in the pictures in your papers today, stood in the front row at the Moscow parade yesterday. I was the number two man under General Clark at the time, and so I saw General Koniev's deputy very often. We saw each other three or four times a week. Over a period of time he outlined his philosophy to me, and it can be summarized as something like this: "You come from a democracy. You're proud of the freedoms which you have. However, you will live to find that those freedoms are divisive. You ask your people to pass on issues which are so complicated that they cannot possibly decide whether the black answer is right or the white answer. And you send them to the polls to vote on those subjects. You're going to find that as time goes on in this jet age—he did not know about the atomic part then—you're going to find that they cannot reach sound decisions. We, in the Soviet Union, however, have solved that problem by appointing wise men at the head who tell our people what to do. We don't ask them. We don't have these foolish voting contests to decide these issues. You might just as well ask your people to vote on whether the Einstein theory is correct or not. What do they know about it?"

His second thesis was this: "You have religion. What a wonderful invention for the capitalists! Of course you want to tell the people to get their reward in heaven, so you can exploit them on this earth. You don't want to give them their just reward here. You have even gone so far as to devise a commandment, 'Thou shalt not steal,' so that they don't get that reward here."

His third thesis was this: "In order to make any government work, the people have to support it energetically, and that requires a very extensive educational campaign. It is necessary to start educating citizens at a very early age."

It is significant that that very officer has been made the head of what is called in the Soviet Union the "Main Political Directorate of the Ministry of Defense." He has about two thousand assistants, many of them university graduates, to help him. His job is to educate the young men of the Soviet armed forces; and because there is a turnover of about two million of them a year, he has a sizable audience. Also, knowing him as I do, knowing how dedicated he is to his cause, I'm sure he's doing a very effective job.

To show you how effective their system is on these young men, I'd like to give you some examples. Mrs. Gruenther and I have two sons, and both of them have served in Korea. One of them was seriously wounded there. That young man, as the head of an infantry company, advanced almost to the Yalu River. Whenever he advanced, he had air support and artillery support and all the assistance that a powerful nation could afford in order to be saving human lives. He was fighting against men, Communists, who had no air support, and when I say no air support, I mean not even one plane was ever put in front of a Communist advance. What did that mean? It meant that they suffered losses five, six, seven times the losses that my son's company had. But those Communist soldiers had a dedication, or a sense of fanaticism, if that is a better explanation, because of their indoctrination, and they kept coming on and on in spite of their terrible losses.

A year ago today we were in the last stages of a struggle in Indo-China where he had at Dien Bien Phu some twelve thousand members of the gallant French Union surrounded by thirty to forty thousand Communist forces. The Communists again had no air support, and again they took terrible losses, but on and on and on they came.

We must find an answer to that fanaticism, but our answer would never—must never—be the same as theirs. However, the problem we face was outlined by this former Soviet friend of mine. We must match their fanaticism by a dedication to our way of life. There is no reason why we should not achieve it. We have everything. We have religion—a wonderful spiritual strength—a sense of freedom, and above all, the dignity of the individual. We have everything that men should be willing to fight for in a hot war or cold war. Our job, as I see it, is to inspire these 400 million people in NATO to be able to continue the struggle, to make the sacrifices which are going to be necessary for an enduring peace. We must understand our responsibilities as well as our privileges.

I do not have the answer to the problem. I feel that I'm much in the same position of an American comedian, who a few years ago said he had the solution to the submarine problem. When asked for this answer, he replied: "Well, it's a very simple thing. All you do is bring the ocean to a boil; that will force the submarines to the top, and when they get there you knock them off!" "Well," someone asked, "how do you get the ocean to a boil?" "Oh," he answered, "now just a second. All I was doing here was outlining the general principle. It's up to you to work out the details."

I, as he did, am submitting the general principle to you, in the belief that this very distinguished group can work out the details. It is, of course, not a military problem. However, unless we solve this problem of public participation, we are not going to succeed in this struggle.

I'd like now to move on to another point. NATO has been accused of being aggressive. That is simply not true. At my headquarters we make the plans for the defense of this part of the world. I can promise you that there has never been as much as one sentence written that envisages that we will start a war. In fact, we go on the assumption that we will have to absorb the first blow. That is a major disadvantage, but I'm sure that it is the right approach. However, we must counter these Soviet charges. For when we convince our people that this is a defensive organization—that NATO is an instrument for peace—I'm sure that we can get them to make the necessary sacrifices and to have the necessary wisdom and perseverance to support an alliance of this character.

No military alliance of this kind has ever succeeded before in peacetime. There were times in the past four years when people said ours would not work. One public figure characterized it as "an administrative monstrosity." My answer to that is that we have made it work. In this, NATO could be likened to the bumblebee. You could prove by logic and aerodynamics that the bumblebee cannot fly—his body is too heavy and his wings are too small. But the bumblebee is too determined to be deterred by logic and aerodynamics, so he goes ahead and flies anyway.

We in NATO have not been deterred by our difficulties, either. We have been able to make this organization succeed. One of the greatest tributes that has been paid to our effectiveness is the fact that the Soviet Union has made the dissolution of NATO the number one objective of Soviet foreign policy. A year ago they even offered to join it, although there may have been a reason why they made the offer on April Fool's day.

I'm not cynical about any efforts for lasting peace. On the contrary, I'm optimistic. I say that our statesmen can find an answer if they receive continuing popular support. We must continue to develop our position of strength, and above all, to improve our unity. I have seen this organization grow from the time it was a gleam in the planner's eye, and to me it is my whole life. I have seen it succeed in spite of numerous frustrations. I'm convinced, in spite of the difficulties still to be overcome, it will thrive.

When General Eisenhower called our staff together four years ago, he told them this: "The outstanding characteristic of an allied staff officer is an ability to have a ready smile." That was his way of stating that friends could work well together; that friends could solve their problems if they had mutual confidence in each other. We have that characteristic in our headquarters, and all of them, including Admiral Fechtoler's headquarters in Naples, are all very happy headquarters. Of course, it is not always easy. Sitting outside of my office is an American sergeant who gets more money than an Italian colonel of thirty years' service. That is the type of irritation we run into, but the Italian colonel feels that he is dedicated to his cause, and he overlooks that type of irritation. With that sort of spirit —with that sort of dedication—it is not possible to contemplate failure.

I want to express my gratitude to the Italian people and the Italian Government for the loyal support they have always given us. With such unity, such understanding, such perseverance, no power, however menacing, will be able to prevail against this alliance.

Mille grazie a tutti per la vostra gentile attenzione. (Thank you very much for your very kind attention.)

NATIONAL IDEALS

A FANFARE FOR PROMETHEUS [1]

LEARNED HAND [2]

Judge Learned Hand, retired Chief Judge of the United States Court of Appeals, one of the nation's leading jurists for many years, gave this address at the Forty-eighth Annual Dinner Meeting, American Jewish Committee, New York City, on January 29, 1955. The speech was in response to the Committee's presentation to Judge Hand of the American Liberties Medallion.

The Judge's theme was that true liberty is based upon the fact that "it is only by trial and error, by insistent scrutiny and by readiness to reexamine presently accredited conclusions that we have risen, so far as in fact we have risen, from our brutish ancestors; and I believe that in our loyalty to these habits lies our only chance, not merely of progress, but even of survival." His thesis, in line with the writings and speeches of Walter Bagehot, John Stuart Mill, and other interpreters of liberty of thought and action, was both timely and significant.

His analysis, organization, ideas and language, enriched by literary-historical allusions, were in true harmony with his reasoning and expression in his long line of judicial writings and speeches. His delivery, as usual, was "measured, but vigorous and lively. At all points he was communicative in spite of his depth of thinking and reference to his manuscript."

The Judge once told a reporter that all his decisions and speeches were written in longhand, "frequently after hours of intense struggle" (*New Yorker,* 20:18-19, June 10, 1944). He never dictates. The Judge deplores the rise of ghost writers and believes that in compositional excellence oratory has declined. In the older days, according to him, orators had more prestige and were "more creative."

Former President James B. Conant of Harvard, in presenting an honorary degree to Judge Hand, said of him, "A judge worthy of his name, judicial in his temper, profound in his knowledge, a philosopher whose decisions affect a nation." [3]

---

[1] Text furnished by the American Jewish Committee, 386 Fourth Avenue, New York 16, New York, and permission for this reprint through the courtesy of Judge Learned Hand.

[2] For biographical note, see Appendix.

[3] For further comment on Learned Hand as a speaker see *Representative American Speeches: 1943-44,* p254-7; *1952-53,* p 121-9.

Mr. Chairman, Ladies and Gentlemen:

I should have to be more than human, if I was not staggered by the terms in which your president announced to me that you proposed to single me out for this unique evidence of your regard. In what I have to say I shall not try to justify him; rather I am going to suggest that you join me in asking what we mean by those "principles of civil liberties and human rights," of which he credits me with being a votary. You will agree, will you not, that we cannot go far in that inquiry until we have achieved some notion of what we mean by Liberty; and that has always proved a hard concept to define. The natural, though naïve, opinion is that it means no more than that each individual shall be allowed to pursue his own desires without let or hindrance; and that, although it is true that this is practically impossible, still it does remain the goal, approach to which measures our success. Why then is not a beehive or an anthill a perfect example of a free society? Surely you have been a curious and amused watcher beside one of these.

In and out of their crowded pueblo the denizens pass in great number, each bent upon his own urgent mission, quite oblivious of all the rest except as he must bend his path to avoid them. It is a scene of strenuous purposeful endeavor in which each appears to be, and no doubt in fact is, accomplishing his own purpose; and yet he is at the same time accomplishing the purpose of the group as a whole. As I have gazed at it, the sentence from the Collect of the Episcopal prayerbook has come to me: "Whose service is perfect freedom."

Why is it then that we so positively rebel against the hive and the hill as a specimen of a free society? Why is it that such prototypes of totalitarianisms arouse our deepest hostility? Unhappily it is not because they cannot be realized; or at least because they cannot be approached, for a substantial period. Who can be sure that such apalling forecasts as Aldous Huxley's *Brave New World*, or Orwell's *1984* are not prophetic? Indeed, there have often been near approaches to such an order. Germany at the end of 1940 was probably not far removed from one; and who of us knows that there are not countless persons, today living within the boundaries of Russia, and perhaps of

China, who are not willing partners, accepting as their personal aspirations the official definitions of the good, the true and the beautiful? Indeed, there have been, and still are, in our own United States large and powerful groups who, if we are to judge their purposes by their conduct, see treason in all dissidence, and would welcome an era in which all of us should think, feel and live in consonance with duly prescribed patterns. Human nature is malleable, especially if you can indoctrinate the disciple with indefectible principles before anyone else reaches him. (I fancy that the Janissaries were as fervent Mohammedans as the authentic Turks.) Indeed, we hear from those who are entitled to an opinion that at times the abject confessions, made in Russia by victims who know that they are already marked for slaughter, are not wrung from them by torture, or threats against their families. Rather they come from partisans, so obsessed with the faith, that, when they are told that the occasion calls for scapegoats and that they have been selected, recognize and assent to the propriety of the demand and cooperate in its satisfaction. It is as though, when the right time comes, the drones agreed to their extinction in the interest of the hive.

Nor need we be surprised that men so often embrace almost any doctrines, if they are proclaimed with a voice of absolute assurance. In a universe that we do not understand, but with which we must in one way or another somehow manage to deal; and aware of the conflicting desires that clamorously beset us, between which we must choose and which we must therefore manage to weigh, we turn in our bewilderment to those who tell us that they have found a path out of the thickets, and possess the scales by which to appraise our needs. Over and over again such prophets succeed in converting us to unquestioning acceptance; there is scarcely a monstrous belief that has not had its day and its passionate adherents, so eager are we for safe footholds in our dubious course. How certain is any one of us that he too might not be content to follow any fantastic creed, if he was satisfied that nothing would ever wake him from the dream? And, indeed, if there were nothing to wake him, how should he distinguish its articles from the authentic dictates of verity? Remember, too, that it is by no means clear that we are happier in the faith we do profess than we should be under the spell of an orthodoxy that was safe against all heresy. Cruel and savage as orthodoxies have always proved to be, the faithful seem able to convince themselves that the heretics, as they continue to crop up, get nothing worse than their due, and to rest with an easy conscience.

In any event my thesis is that the best answer to such systems is not so much in their immoral quality—immoral though they may be—as in the fact that they are inherently unstable, because they are at war with our only trustworthy way of living in accord with the facts. For I submit that it is only by trial and error, by insistent scrutiny and by readiness to reexamine presently accredited conclusions that we have risen, so far as in fact we have risen, from our brutish ancestors; and I believe that in our loyalty to these habits lies our only chance, not merely of progress, but even of survival. They were not indeed a part of our aboriginal endowment: Man, as he emerged, was not prodigally equipped to master the infinite diversity of his environment. Obviously, enough of us did manage to get through; but it has been a statistical survival, for the individual's native powers of adjustment are by no means enough for his personal safety, any more than are those of other creatures. The precipitate of our experience is far from absolute verity; and our exasperated resentment at all dissent is a sure index of our doubts. Take, for instance, our constant recourse to the word, "subversive," as a touchstone of impermissible deviation from accepted canons. All discussion, all debate, all dissidence tends to question, and in consequence to upset, existing convictions: that is precisely its purpose and its justification. He is, indeed, a "subversive" who disputes those precepts that I most treasure and seeks to persuade me to substitute his own. He may have no shadow of desire to resort to anything but persuasion; he may be of those to whom any forcible sanction of conformity is anathema; yet it remains true that he is trying to bring about my apostasy, and I hate him just in proportion as I fear his success. Contrast this protective resentment with the assumption that lies at the base of our whole system that the best chance for truth to emerge is a fair field for all ideas. Nothing, I submit, more completely betrays our latent disloyalty to this premise to all that we pretend to believe, than the increasingly common resort to this and other question-begging words. Their imprecision comforts us by enabling us to suppress arguments that disturb our complacency, and yet to continue to congratulate ourselves on keeping the faith as we have received it from the Founding Fathers.

Heretics have been hateful from the beginning of recorded time; they have been ostracized, exiled, tortured, maimed and butchered; but it has generally proved impossible to smother them; and when it has not, the society that has succeeded has always declined. Façades of authority, however imposing, do not survive after it has appeared that they rest upon the sands of human conjecture and compromise. And so, if I am to say what are "the principles of civil liberties and human right," I answer that they lie in habits, customs—conventions, if you will—that tolerate dissent, and can live without irrefragable certainties; that are ready to overhaul existing assumptions; that recognize that we never see save through a glass, darkly; and that at long last we shall succeed only so far as we continue to undertake "the intolerable labor of thought"—that most distasteful of all our activities. If such a habit and such a temper pervade a society, it will not need institutions to protect its "civil liberties and human right"; so far as they do not, I venture to doubt how far anything else can protect them: whether it be bills of rights, or courts that must in the name of interpretation read their meaning into them.

This may seem to you a bleak and cheerless conclusion, too alien to our nature to be practical. "We must live from day to day"—you will say—"to live is to act, and to act is to choose and decide. How can we carry on at all without some principles, some patterns to meet the conflicts in which each day involves us?" Indeed, we cannot, nor am I suggesting that we should try; but I am suggesting that it makes a vital difference —the vital difference—whether we deem our principles and our patterns to be eternal verities, rather than the best postulates so far attainable. Was it not Holmes who said: "The highest courage is to stake everything on a premise you know tomorrow's evidence may disprove"? "Ah"—you will reply—"there's the

rub. That may be the highest courage, but how many have it?
You are hopelessly wrong, if you assume the general prevalence
of such a virtue; ordinary men must be given more than conjec-
tures, if they are to face grave dangers." But do you really
believe that? Do you not see about you every day and everywhere the precise opposite? Not alone on the battlefield; but
in the forest, the desert and the plain; in the mountains, at sea,
on the playing field, even in the laboratory and the factory,—
yes (do not laugh) at the card table and the race track—men
are forever putting it "upon the touch to win or lose it all."
Without some smack of uncertainty and danger, to most of us
the world would be a tepid, pallid show. Surely, like me, you
have all felt something of this, when you have looked on those
pathetic attempts to depict in paint or stone the delights of
Paradise. I own that the torments of Hell never fail to horrify
me; not even the glee of the demons in charge is an adequate
relief, though the artist has generally been successful in giving
a veracious impression of the gusto with which they discharge
their duties. But when I turn to the Congregation of the
Blessed, I cannot avoid a sense of anticlimax; strive as I may,
the social atmosphere seems a bit forced; and I recall those very
irreverent verses of Lowes Dickinson:

> Burning at first no doubt would be worse,
> But time the impression would soften,
> While those who are bored with praising the Lord,
> Would be more bored with praising Him often.

By some happy fortuity man is a projector, a designer, a
builder, a craftsman; it is among his most dependable joys to
impose upon the flux that passes before him some mark of himself, aware though he always must be of the odds against him.
His reward is not so much in the work as in its making; not so
much in the prize as in the race. We may win when we lose, if
we have done what we can; for by so doing we have made
real at least some part of that finished product in whose fabri-
cation we are most concerned—ourselves. And if at the end
some friendly critic shall pass by and say: "My friend, how
good a job do you really think you have made of it all?" we

can answer: "I know as well as you that it is not of high quality; but I did put into it whatever I had, and that was the game I started out to play." It is still in the lap of the gods whether a society can succeed, based on "civil liberties and human rights," conceived as I have tried to describe them; but of one thing at least we may be sure: the alternatives that have so far appeared, have been immeasurably worse; and so, whatever the outcome, I submit to you that we must press along. Borrowing from Epictetus, let us say to ourselves: "Since we are men, we will play the part of a Man;" and how can I better end than by recalling to you the concluding passage of *Prometheus Unbound?*

> To suffer woes which Hope thinks infinite;
> To forgive wrongs darker than death or night;
> To defy Power, which seems omnipotent;
> To love, and bear; to hope till Hope creates
> From its own wreck the thing it contemplates;
> Neither to change, nor falter, nor repent;
> This, like thy glory, Titan, is to be
> Good, great and joyous, beautiful and free;
> This is alone Life, Joy, Empire and Victory.

WHAT IS A FREE SOCIETY? [4]

Robert J. Blakely [5]

Robert J. Blakely, manager of the Central Regional Office of the Fund for Adult Education of the Ford Foundation, gave this address at the opening session of the seventeenth annual National Farm Institute, February 18, 1955, at the Hotel Fort Des Moines, Iowa.

The theme of this two day Institute, sponsored by the Greater Des Moines Chamber of Commerce, was "The Farmer and Free Society." Other speakers were President Virgil Hancher of the State University of Iowa, Barbara Ward Jenkinson, of the staff of the London *Economist*, Herbert Brownell, United States Attorney General, Sir Roger Makins, British Ambassador to the United States, Harold Stassen, Director of Foreign Operations Administration, and other leaders in agriculture, labor, foreign trade, and international affairs.

This address is characteristic of Mr. Blakely's methods of speech composition, and reflects his impatience with surface examination of contemporary problems. Rather, in his public addresses he attempts to reconstruct the philosophical backgrounds of man and his strivings—to interpret them as revealed in historical, cultural, literary, political, economic, and esthetic utterances and conduct. The speaker coins aphorisms, continually reframes concepts in original terms, yet adopts a style brisk, terse, and provocative. (Note his various uses of interrogation, and sometimes his abrupt personal conclusions.) His style is that of enlightened journalism. (He was formerly editorial writer on the Des Moines *Register* and the St. Louis *Star Times*.) He has a mature understanding of traditional literature and thought, but at every point he is alert to the issues and conditions of the hour.

Mr. Blakely has been in constant demand as a speaker. He has talked often over the radio, before popular audiences as well as before national professional associations. Especially since his appointment as regional manager of the Fund for Adult Education has he addressed professional and lay audiences. His favorite theme has been continuation education as basic for the survival and progress of the free American (and world) civilization.[6]

Today the nucleus of the atom is both split and fused, but man is only split and confused. In this situation, what is the

[4] Text supplied and permission for this reprinting through the courtesy of Robert J. Blakely.

[5] For biographical note, see Appendix.

[6] For further comment on Robert J. Blakely as speaker see *Representative American Speeches: 1945-46*, p241-61; *1951-52*, p 152-61.

meaning of a free society? The question forces us to be philosophical. We have to ask other questions: What is a free man? And, indeed, What is man?

Man, by his own modest admission, is the highest form of life, and life is part of the physical universe. The essential difference between nonorganic and organic matter is that organisms have purposes. Life evolves by "the gradual unfoldment and increase of organisms' purposes. The evolution of species is a series of successive plant or animal inventions for new purposes. . . ." [7] Man is the inheritor of an incredibly long accumulation of biological inventions: the circulatory system, the internal skeleton, the lungs, the eye. We cannot touch a member, think of an organ or reflect on a process of the human body that is not triumphant and wonderful. As a result he is the most highly adaptable form of life. Age after age, in all parts of the planet, in all kinds of circumstances, he is tough and resourceful. He has even invented a new kind of evolution.

Man makes the tools and machines that make further physical evolution unnecessary. Does he want to hunt like the bear? He invents the spear. Does he want to dive like the fish? He invents the submarine. Does he want to fly like the bird? He invents the airplane. There is no end in sight: Yet he himself remains unspecialized. He takes on and puts off at will the specialized organs and capacities that encumber the bear, the whale and the eagle.

To do all this man had to become social. This meant language and culture. Language and culture meant something astoundingly new—the transmission of experience and knowledge. What one man discovered, all men could learn. What one generation accomplished, the next could build upon. So within the past ten thousand years man's inventions have blossomed—agriculture, the domestication of animals, writing, metalworking. With these and other inventions taking care of his concerns as an animal, man turned to his concerns as a human being—through myth, religion, art, literature.

All this has tremendous implications.

[7] Weston La Barre, *The Human Animal* (University of Chicago Press, 1954), p4.

First, the evolution of man is in his own mind and hands: second, the process is social, not solitary. Third, human society has become the most important part of the individual's environment.

Here we must look at what the anthropologists call "culture." A culture is a pattern of life that is learned and shared. I repeat that culture is learned. Compare the newly-born human with the newly-hatched ant. The child is helpless, knowing how only to cry for help. The ant is fully competent, going at once about its duties. But the ant, needing to learn little, can learn little, and the child, needing to learn much, can learn much. The individual learns his behavior from his culture. Because man is biologically unspecialized, there is a bewildering variety of cultures, and each is expressive of only a small part of the potentialities of man.

Man can reflect on his individual potentialities that are denied by his culture. He can reflect on the differences between cultures. It was inevitable, therefore, that some time men would begin to question the magic that surrounded their customs, that they would begin to discuss and criticize, that they would assert their individuality and try to reform and improve society.

In Western civilization, this began with the Greeks. The reactions were two, illustrated by Athens and Sparta. In Athens began the tradition of the free society—a society open to new possibilities, a society encouraging its citizens to be "open selves."

Even today, probably the best definition of the free society is that given by Pericles in his funeral oration.

Our constitution does not copy the laws of neighboring states; we are rather a pattern to others than imitators ourselves. Its administration favors the many instead of the few; this is why it is called a democracy. If we look to the laws, they afford equal justice to all in their private differences; if to social standing, advancement in public life falls to reputation for capacity, class considerations not being allowed to interfere with merit; nor again does poverty bar the way, if a man is able to serve the state, he is not hindered by the obscurity of his condition. The freedom which we enjoy in our government extends also to our ordinary life. There, far from exercising a jealous surveillance over each other, we do not feel called upon to be angry with our neighbor for doing what he likes, or even to indulge in those injurious looks which cannot fail to be offensive, although they inflict no positive penalty. But all this ease in our private relations does not make us lawless as citizens. Against this fear is our chief safeguard, teaching us to obey the magistrates and the laws, particularly such as regard the protection of the injured, whether they are actually on the statute book, or belong to that code which, although unwritten, yet cannot be broken without acknowledged disgrace. . . .

If we turn to our military policy, there also we differ from our antagonists. We throw open our city to the world, and never by alien acts exclude foreigners from any opportunity of learning or observing, although the eyes of an enemy may occasionally profit by our liberality; trusting less in system and policy than to the native spirit of our citizens; while in education, where our rivals from their very cradles by a painful discipline seek after manliness, at Athens we live exactly as we please, and yet are just as ready to encounter every legitimate danger. . . .

Our public men have, besides politics, their private affairs to attend to, and our ordinary citizens, though occupied with the pursuits of industry, are still fair judges of public matters; for, unlike any other nation, regarding him who takes no part in these duties not as unambitious but as useless, we Athenians are able to judge at all events if we cannot originate, and instead of looking on discussion as a stumbling-block in the way of action, we think it an indispensable preliminary to any wise action at all.

The breakdown of the tribal society, where custom is unquestioned and authority is taken for granted, was and is a painful experience—perhaps like the trauma of birth for the individual. It dissolves the organic unity of society. It requires personal responsibility. It sets up abstract relations where before there were personal and family relations. In exchange for the open possibilities of self and society it demands a heavy price of understanding, reasonableness, voluntary cooperation. Strife and conflict become familiar; accommodation and compromise become required.

Not surprisingly, therefore, another reaction toward the breakdown of the spontaneous tribal society was to establish a contrived tribal society—to substitute manufactured magic, to use reason to suppress reason, to use the potentialities of the state to repress potentialities of the individual.

The policies of Sparta were: (1) Keep out foreign influences; (2) wage war against all equalitarian, democratic and individualistic ideas; (3) be independent in trade; (4) uphold the differences between your tribe and others; between superiors and inferiors; (5) dominate and enslave your neighbors.

The Greeks identified four main forms of government, and these are still useful to consider today. A quick review will underline the nature of a free society.

1. Under a tyranny, the ruler uses his absolute power for his own good. This is too crude for our sophisticated age. But the issue remains. Modern tyranny rests on the premise that the state is the end and the citizen the means. The fact that the ultimate welfare of the citizen is pretended to be the goal of the state changes nothing. Absolute power is used by a few individuals for their own good, identified with the state, and individuals are used as means.

2. The benevolent despot accepts the good of the governed as the proper aim of the state. But he maintains that he is best qualified to rule for them and resists any limitations on his authority. We have seen this in modern Turkey and in several Latin American countries. We must not underrate the difficulty of the transition to self-government. Nevertheless, historical experience justifies several statements. No human being, unrestricted, can be counted on not to abuse his power. No human being, however virtuous, can be wise enough to choose various things for others better than they can choose for themselves. No human being lives forever, and in a despotism no rule can provide for a virtuous and wise successor. Finally, people can learn how to govern themselves only by assuming responsibilities.

3. An oligarchy accepts men as ends and accepts a government of law. But it insists that only the few can exercise suffrage. Let us be grateful for certain oligarchies in the past, including that which established the American republic. But again, certain statements must be made. Just as no individual can be trusted to be all wise and all virtuous, neither can any class. And what is to be the basis of the oligarchy? We in the modern world know too much about the effects of heredity and environment to accept the two traditional bases of oligarchy—family and wealth. We know how nature scatters her talents at random. We know well how people are corrupted when they rule others and how they are stunted when they are ruled by others. Again human

beings can learn how to govern themselves only by assuming the responsibility to do so.

This puts us up squarely against certain basic problems of freedom in a democracy.

1. Do we mean freedom under law or freedom from law? Can a democratic government do anything, anything at all, provided it is with majority consent and constitutional approval? Or can even majority rule and constitutional sanction be bad? Is freedom to do what one wants to do or what one ought to do? My answer is that freedom is to do what one ought to do, but he must discover it himself. This means the freedom to err and to learn from error. A majority cannot be trusted to be all virtuous and all wise. A majority can be the worst tyrant of all, because it holds social approbation and ostracism in one hand and force in the other. A majority can be wrong. A minority can be right. Right or wrong a minority represents the rights of all minorities, which make up a society. A minority is a touchstone, a gadfly, a stimulus for reappraisal.

2. A necessary complement of political freedom is economic freedom. Economic freedom is economic self-government, control of one's labor. What does this mean when huge organizations of capital and labor confront each other? When government intervention is pervasive because of defense, the need to avoid depression and the demands of equity? The United States from its very beginning was a mixture of private enterprise and public enterprise. Socialism is no longer just a theory; it is a reality. It too turns out to be a mixture of private enterprise and public enterprise. The question is, How can private enterprise and public enterprise be made to run in harness instead of pulling against each other? This is a practical, not a theoretical matter. At the bottom are decisions to be made by each person in privacy and honesty: It is the objective economic or political in disguise? Is the goal an increase in the general wealth or an increase in special advantage? Can the few judge for the many better than the many can judge for themselves? Can the many be counted on to understand and advance the general welfare? The objective of the economic system is the creation of wealth, and the objective of wealth in a free society

is to increase the freedom of the individual. The individual can learn responsibility only by exercising responsibility. The intrusion of government into economic affairs is only one way—and often not the best way—of extending democratic control over businesses and unions. Another way is extension from "beneath" —the consumers, the employees, the union members, the stockholders. For too long we have pretended that our economic system was a separate compartment of life. We can afford to do so no longer.

3. Does freedom of expression help or hinder the pursuit of truth? Here we have an increasingly drastic contrast between our professions and our practices. The professions of a free society can still stir our blood—the organ voices of Milton and Locke, of Jefferson and Mill, of Holmes and Hand. Truth will triumph if it is free to combat error; falsehood is best combatted by free discussion; we are not God—we do not know the truth; even if we did, suppression would be wrong, wrong for the suppressors, who cannot be trusted to limit their suppressions to error; wrong for the suppressed, who may be right, and even if wrong cannot learn from their error. In the words of Milton,

> Since, therefore, the knowledge and survey of vice is in this world so necessary to the constituting of human virtue, and the scanning of error to the confirmation of truth, how can we more safely, and with less danger, scout into the regions of sin and falsity than by reading all manners of tractates and hearing all manners of reasoning?

But the issue is not resolved. James Fitzjames Stephen put it, "Speculation on government, morals and religion is a matter of vital practical importance, and not food for mere curiosity." Milton would have censored "Popish tractates." Cromwell, who cried to the Presbyterian prelates, "Brethren, by the bowels of Christ, I beseech you to think that you might be wrong!" did not think that he himself could be wrong. Holmes enunciated the doctrine of "clear and present danger" to justify restriction of speech. And in our time we have experienced an increasing constriction of civil liberties—in the name of securing those liberties. We have seen public opinion used to bludgeon down dissent, difference, inquiry.

Speculation is a matter of vital practical importance, in both ways—the abuses and the uses. The dangers are double-edged. Believers in freedom have always felt that the dangers of lack of freedom have been greater than the dangers of freedom. This is so because the use of freedom can be educative, while the curbing of freedom is a blighting and a corruption.

4. This leads us to the problem of security. Practically there are always restrictions on freedom. One reason is that various freedoms collide. Another reason is that at various times and places, there are differing degrees of permissible error. What is the best way to avoid error—by freedom or restriction of freedom? Is it not through the freedom to inquire, question, challenge and pose alternatives? If legislators need freedom to know and discuss in order to legislate wisely, do not those who elect the legislators and determine the climate within which policy is made also need freedom to know and discuss? And against whom are we trying to secure ourselves? The enemy or our own people? Are we afraid of the writer or the reader? The speaker or the listener? Are we merely against slavery from people who are different from ourselves in race and nationality? Or are we against slavery?

During World War II Elmer Davis, director of the Office of War Information, outlined what he called "The Strategy of Truth." Since we were killing and dying, for our cause, should we balk at lying? Not if it served our purpose. We were not "sicklied o'er with the pale cast of thought" and enervated by moral queasiness. But lying would not serve our purpose. Our cause and our purpose were such as to require and be best served by the strategy of truth. The strategy of truth is a part of the strategy of freedom, which is best served by the exercise of freedom.

I have been trying to state classic issues in the light of modern conditions. It is time to understand better several of the forces behind these conditions.

Let us return to an earlier point: Man is in charge of his own evolution; this evolution is social, not solitary; and human society is the most important part of human environment. During the last three hundred years man's control over his physical environment has been rising—not in a straight line, but in a line curving upward. Within the lifetime of some of us in this room he will probably send explorers outside the dominion of earth's gravity.

This phenomenal increase in power over the physical world has meant also a phenomenal increase in power over human beings. Society has long been man's most important environment. There is a difference now—a greater intensity, an all-embraciveness; all parts of our lives and all peoples are caught up in intimate interdependency. All human beings, not just those of his own culture, are now the most important part of each person's environment. All human beings *together*, not in isolated cultures, now hold in their hands the evolution of human life.

We are one another's physical environment. We are also fellow humans. In which of these two ways will we regard one another? If as physical environment, we will engage in a ruthless endless battle to destroy, exploit, and manipulate one another. If as fellow humans, we will share respect, purposes and power. I soberly believe that this is the issue we cannot escape—a descent into depths of bestiality such as only man is capable of or an ascent to a much higher plane of relationships between individuals and peoples.

Greek civilization faced and failed this test. Listen to Thucydides describing Hellas at the end of the fifth year of the Peloponnesian war.

Words had to change their ordinary meaning and to take that which was now given them. Reckless audacity came to be considered the courage of a loyal ally; prudent hesitation, specious cowardice; moderation was held to be a cloak for unmanliness; ability to see all sides of a question inaptness to act on any. Frantic violence became the attribute of manliness; cautious plotting, a justifiable means of self-defense. The advocate of extreme measures was always trustworthy; his opponent a man to be suspected. To succeed in a plot was to have a shrewd head, to divine a plot a still shrewder; but to try to provide against having to do either was to break up your party and to be afraid of your adversaries. In fine, to forestall an intending criminal, or to suggest the idea of a crime where it was wanting, was equally commended, until even blood became a weaker tie than party, from the superior readiness of those united by the latter to dare everything without reserve; for such associations had not in view the blessings derivable from established institutions but were formed by ambition for their overthrow; and the confidence of their members in each other rested less on any religious sanction than upon complicity in crime.

Today we face the issue grown gigantically greater in scope and penetration. Not merely the eastern Mediterranean but all the planet is involved. Not the future of a single civilization but the continuity of human society is at stake. You know that I could put this even more strongly. I shall not. We must recognize the possibilities, perhaps even the probabilities, but terror is no friend even of survival and much less of freedom.

If we clear our heads of terror, we will see that it is the struggle for freedom that is shaking the world. In Mohammedan myth a jinni is a spirit lower than the angels capable of appearing in human and animal forms and influencing mankind for good and evil. Two jinn have been let out of the bottle, and they cannot be put back. One jinni is the idea that the individual human being matters. The other is that man can do something about his condition, with respect both to physical nature and to society. These are crude. They can influence and be commanded to do terrible things. But they are also the raw materials of human dignity, a respect for self and others, and self-government under law and justice. They are abroad in the world like the radiation from nuclear explosions.

These jinn were first let out of the bottle by Western civilization. In the West they have achieved their greatest triumphs for good. In the West also the strains of the open society have been the greatest—the demands for personal responsibility, for reason, for understanding, for maturity; the abstractness, the impersonalness, the loneliness.

The modern closed society is a deliberate attempt to return to the womb of the tribal society. But innocence lost cannot be regained. All spontaneity is gone. The planks of policy in the contrived closed society of Sparta describe fairly well policies of modern totalitarian societies. The ideologies of imperialistic Japan, Fascist Italy and Nazi Germany had little universal appeal. This is not true of the ideology of Communist Russia. For the first time since the Renaissance the Western ideology of freedom has serious competition from another source. This is a far more serious matter than the Emperor's navy and the *Wehrmacht*. How can the universalist appeal of Russian communism be explained? It is a bogus version of certain key ideas of the West, turned against the West, like the guns of Napoleon, because of the West's shortcomings, hypocrisies, abuses and delays.

Let us not so misunderstand the situation as to think of the world-wide issue as being between two halves of the world— the Communist and the free. The issue is one of many worlds, many peoples, all striving to be free as nations and to become freer as individuals. These peoples will ally themselves or keep themselves neutral as they think bests fits their interests, the same way the American people have done. We, the American people, who had a "neutrality act" when World War II began, should not find it difficult to understand the neutralist policies of statesmen like Nehru.

We will be able to gather around us and hold the support of the peoples of the world only by demonstrating a moral superiority over our enemies. We can demonstrate this only by exemplifying at home the free way of life we say we stand for, by giving aid to other peoples in advancing their freedom, and by respecting their right to be different from ourselves.

Atomic stalemate between the United States and the USSR is now a fact. Other mysterious weapons of mass destruction are wrapped in secrecy, but we know they exist. The rulers of the Soviet Union and Red China seem to be uncompromising. There are officials even in the United States who seem to be courting a war. The United States has two allies, Rhee and Chiang, who have a vested interest in a world war. Ahead looms the day when even immature governments like those of Costa Rica and Guatemala will have weapons of mass destruction. I must confess I do not see how another general war will be averted. But somehow, somehow it must be averted.

Suppose our hopes are realized. Suppose war is averted. Suppose even the Soviet system collapses or is transformed. What about the long road ahead? Do we seriously believe that the peoples of the world are going to cease striving for self-government, for an improvement in their personal and social conditions? Do we seriously believe that other spurious doctrines and false champions will not arise if there is not hope for a better life given through the leadership of those who respect human worth? Where is the hope if American people do not take to their hearts again the cause of the "tired, the poor, the huddled masses yearning to breathe free"? This is not new. Jefferson wrote of and for all men. Franklin thought in terms of the world. Lincoln brooded about "this nation or any nation so conceived and so dedicated."

What is new is a keener awareness at the same time of the incredible variety of ways of life and of the underlying sameness of man; of our various expressions and our common themes; of our common nature and predicament.

What is new is a dawning awareness of the possibilities of plenty, of making food and clothing directly from the elements, of domesticating microorganisms as long ago we learned to domesticate animals and plants, of extracting minerals directly from the inexhaustible resources of the sea, of using energy directly from the sun.

What is new is promising insights into the nature of man and society, which can be used for humane purposes if we are good and wise enough.

What we need is largeness of mind and soul.

Differing civilizations have met many times in the past. Always there have been collisions. Sometimes there have been creations of larger conceptions concerning the possibilities of human life—religions, philosophies, art, science. Few if any of those living in the times of creation could sense what was under way. Perhaps the creations of our anguished time will be equal to the scope and intimacy of the present meeting.

Here and there over the globe men are working feverishly to send rockets beyond the earth's atmosphere—with devices at first and later with crews. Characteristically the major objective is military—a satellite outpost for reconnaissance and the launching of weapons, a backward-looking at destruction, like Lot's wife. But who can tell what this may mean? We may reconnoiter better than we know. For the first time man will be able to get away from our Earth and look upon the cosmos bare, undimmed and undistorted by our filming atmosphere. Perhaps his is what is needed to give us perspective and proportion—to grasp the lonely brotherhood of man in immensity.

When man escapes from gravity, his space ship will be a part of himself—its casing his skin, its air his life. He will be like the first amphibian crawling out of the ocean, taking a private sea within himself. The consequences of the adventure into space could be as unpredictable and as far-reaching as the ascent from the sea, perhaps particularly revolutionary in man's understanding of his nature and his purpose.

As an act of will I refuse to despair. I believe that the drive toward reason and freedom is of the essence of human nature. I believe that mankind has only begun to discover his possibilities, only begun to enunciate the purposes that will help each to fulfill himself by helping others to fulfill themselves, only begun to create the kind of open society that will elicit the almost infinite potentialities of the open self.

I believe in the American people. I believe that in the years ahead we will make of ourselves and help others make of themselves what is called for in this dread and thrilling time.

In the last year we have seen clearly the nature and requirements of freedom. We are learning again first-hand, as our forefathers learned, that freedom is not a luxury, like cake, to be foresworn when times are hard. Instead, freedom is meat and bread, drink and breath, most needed when danger is most clear and closely present. Freedom is dangerous, because life is dangerous. But freedom is the lesser danger than the lack of freedom.

What are the alternatives to a free society? Do you see them? Do you find hope anywhere except in the free way of life that we have imperfectly applied? It can be said of freedom, as of the Golden Rule, that it was not tried and found wanting; instead, it was tried and found difficult.

None of us can know whether the idea of a free society will meet the present test. No more could those in the past. Both faith and despair have been justified and betrayed many times. "We must press along," Judge Learned Hand wrote recently, in his eighty-fourth year, quoting Epictetus, "Since we are men we will play the part of men."

REMARKS ON JEFFERSON DAY [8]

BOWER ALY [9]

Professor Bower Aly, of the Speech Department of the University of Missouri, gave these out-of-doors remarks on the campus of the University of Missouri on April 13, 1955. The occasion was the observance of the 212th anniversary of the birth of Thomas Jefferson. The ceremony was held at Jefferson's original monument, unveiled on this campus on July 4, 1885. Classes were dismissed so that students and faculty could attend the exercises, which are held there each year on April 13.

This speaker's habits of speech composition and delivery were well illustrated in these remarks. Dr. Aly's invention and appeals are based upon broad and liberal intellectual resources. His academic training culminated in a degree at Teachers College, Columbia University, where he specialized in speech education, public address, and rhetoric.

For many years he has taught speech at Missouri, directed graduate studies in the history and criticism of American public address, and published in the area of general speech and forensic speaking. In 1944 he was president of the Speech Association of America and in 1951-1953 he was editor of the *Quarterly Journal of Speech*. His educational philosophy, as this address suggests, is heavily motivated by concepts of political and intellectual liberty, and specifically by postulates of maximum freedom of press and speech.

Dr. Aly's compositional style, not marked by Aristotelian ornamentation or journalistic briskness, is nevertheless condensed, uncomplicated, vigorous, and undisguised in its direction. His style is distinctly Contemporary American (in a good sense) more than Asiatic, Rhodian, or Attic.

Although he prepares his speech manuscripts carefully, he almost invariably speaks extemporaneously and with sufficient vocal liveliness and variety to communicate with much effectiveness both to large open-air or lecture-room groups as well as to radio audiences.

Mr. Chairman: We have come this morning to do honor to Thomas Jefferson, author of the Declaration of American Independence, and of the Statute of Virginia for Religious Freedom, and Father of the University of Virginia. We have come to

[8] Text furnished by Dr. Loren Reid, of the University of Missouri, and permission for this reprint through the courtesy of Dr. Bower Aly.

[9] For biographical note, see Appendix.

honor him, even though we realize that his fame has long since passed beyond our power to praise. Indeed, this morning it behooves us to ask ourselves the searching question whether we are worthy to praise him.

Thomas Jefferson declared eternal warfare against every form of tyranny over the minds of men. In this generation we have quietly witnessed an onslaught on our liberties by those whose plan of attack on Russian tyranny begins with the destruction of American liberty. Are we worthy to praise Thomas Jefferson?

Thomas Jefferson believed in the Constitution, under which he served, and in the Bill of Rights, in which were embodied his ideas of liberty under law. Today we sit complacently while those who would destroy our Bill of Rights slander the precious Fifth Amendment by attaching to it the epithet "Communist." Are we worthy to praise Thomas Jefferson?

Thomas Jefferson welcomed honest dissent boldly expressed as the surest evidence of liberty prevailing. Today we see timid men fleeing to conform; and we witness citizens as yet unconvicted of any crime harried by government informers and suborners of perjury who gain their fees, without our protest, from taxes we have paid. Are we worthy to praise Thomas Jefferson?

In an age which, like our own, knew grave danger, Thomas Jefferson and his contemporaries cast out fear and stood unafraid. Americans today, though rich and powerful, stand irresolute and fearful when they should be confident and strong. Are we worthy to praise Thomas Jefferson?

Mr. Chairman: We Americans of this generation did not earn our liberties. We merely inherited them. We inherited them with our Constitution, our Bill of Rights, and our government of free men established by Washington, Hamilton, and Jefferson. We stand in present danger of being disinherited. No less a person than the Chief Justice of the Supreme Court of the United States has recently warned us of the grave and growing dangers to our ancient liberties. We shall be disinherited unless we learn how to defend the values handed down to us by Jefferson and his compatriots.

Mr. Chairman: I submit that we Americans today have not kept faith with Thomas Jefferson. Since we have not kept true faith with him in our deeds we have no right to praise him with our words. I propose, therefore, that we offer as our tribute today a solemn and inward determination so to live in protest against every form of tyranny that our actions may earn for us the right to praise Jefferson in happier days to come.

THE GENIUS OF DEMOCRACY [10]

LYNN HAROLD HOUGH [11]

Dr. Lynn Harold Hough gave this address in the auditorium of the National Archives, Washington, D.C., depository of the documents that are the basis of this nation's democratic institutions, at the final 1955 meeting of the Washington Pilgrimage, May 1, 1955.

The text as reported in the *Congressional Record* was slightly expanded in delivery.

The speaker had had long experience as scholar, writer on philosophical and religious subjects, preacher, and professor of homiletics and theology (ordained in the Methodist Church).

His educational training and development included his studies at Drew Theological Seminary, postgraduate work at New York University. Beginning in a small church in New Jersey in 1898, he held pastorates in Baltimore, Brooklyn, Detroit, and at the American Church (Presbyterian) in Montreal. He taught historical theology at Garrett Biblical Institute and in 1919 was president of Northwestern University. His later active career included his extended teaching of homiletics at Drew, where he contributed much to the training of hundreds of prospective ministers. In the midst of these speaking activites he published, during forty years, some forty books.

His address at the climax of the Washington Pilgrimage contains in epitome much of the speaker's political-ethical-religious philosophy. His highly condensed utterance, illustrated from the political documents of the American heritage and the secular and religious thinking of the Hebraic-Christian tradition, focused upon the problem of individual self-realization in relation to statism. According to him, "The dignity of man is the glory of God," furnishes the constructive principle by which is resolved the dilemma of man as a political-social-moral being.

Dr. Hough is a master of speech construction and language usage. In the pulpit his reasoning and appeals have been expressed in dynamic delivery—often free from close following of his manuscript or notes.

The theory and the practice of democracy are based upon a sense of the significance of the individuals. Something like six hundred years before the coming of the Christian era the principle was announced dramatically by the two Old Testament

---

[10] Text supplied through the courtesy of Dr. Lynn Harold Hough, with permission for this reprint. For original text see *Congressional Record* 88:(daily) A4278-9. June 15, 1955.

[11] For biographical note, see Appendix.

prophets Jeremiah and Ezekiel. The people felt that they were caught in the evil coming down from their ancestors. They said bitterly "The fathers have eaten sour grapes and the children's teeth are set on edge." This attitude was sharply condemned by the prophets. As Ezekiel put it: "This proverb shall no more be used by you in Israel. Behold all souls are mine, the soul of the father as well as the soul of the son is mine; the soul that sins shall die." Every individual soul has its own standing before God because all belong to Him. A man is never lost in the bundle of life. Here we have the religious basis for democracy—to use terms belonging to a far later time. In the declaration that every individual soul belongs to God you have the charter of democracy.

In the fifth century B. C. you have an expression of what may be called the secular conception of the value of the individual. The philosopher Protagoras declared that the individual man is the measure of all things. Truth must be approached through the individual. He sets the standard. Not because of what he is to God but because of what he is to himself he is important. But here a problem emerges. If the individual is the standard of truth there will be as many kinds of truth as there are individuals. And that means anarchy. In fact this is just what Proudhon, the founder of philosophical anarchy—who was born in the year of the birth of Abraham Lincoln and died in the same year as the death of Lincoln—declared. The danger of the position of Protagoras was clearly seen by Socrates, who made the class rather than the individual standard. Mankind rather than the individual became the standard. And Plato put this conception at the very heart of his conception of the eternal ideas. The two conceptions have been fighting ever since. In the Middle Ages the State was considered more real than the individual citizen, the Church was more real than the individual Christian. In fact the individual was only real as a part of something greater than himself. When the great door of history swung on its hinges the individual was seen in the sharper fashion. So the battles between the absolute state and the individual claiming his rights began. Each principle had something important and true in it. The one alone meant tyranny. The other alone meant lawlessness. The two must be brought together. So democracy began to be seen as involving these larger relationships. We may illustrate the result by a consideration of the circle and the ellipse. Democracy is not a circle with the state at the center. It cannot make terms with tyranny. Democracy is not a circle with the individual at the center. It cannot allow itself to be reduced to anarchy. It is an ellipse with two foci. One focus is the individual. The other focus is the state. They are in equal emphasis. The individual is given all the freedom he can receive without interfering with the common good. The state is given all the power it can exercise without crushing the individual. The legitimate rights of the individual must be maintained.

In America the Declaration of Independence was a great document in the name of individual rights and freedom. The Constitution of the United States is a great document relating the rights of the individual to those of the Federal Government. The two political parties have built themselves about the two principles. One has emphasized the individual man and the individual state. The other has represented the doctrine of central and federal authority. But it must be observed that when in power, the party of the individual usually exercises far reaching central control. And whichever party is out of power becomes the watchful critic of federal exercise of power. Both principles are needed. And together they make a great federal republic which duly recognizes the rights of the individual man and the individual state. On this side of the Atlantic there was a situation where only property owners could vote. There was a situation where only church members could vote. And of course there was the long period when only men could vote. The full recognition of the rights of the individual human being came slowly.

Industrial democracy brings up all the complicated problems of the employer and the employed. Collective bargaining is an attempt to take account of the rights of each. But there is a third factor in the matter of industrial democracy. This involves the consideration of the rights of the general public. Really democratic bargaining would include not merely a struggle between the employer and the employed but it would bring in a representative of the public. This would bring about a more definite approach to justice. Democracy does not mean life lived on a dead level where everybody is comfortable. It takes account of mountains. But it does away with artificial barriers. Anybody who will pay the price of self-discipline and industry is allowed to climb.

Intellectual democracy recognizes differences in the mental capacities of men. But it does mean the right of every man to make the most of the powers of his mind. It seeks out the poor inglorious Miltons and it makes it possible for them to enter into their intellectual heritage.

Spiritual democracy means that no man has a right to obstruct the path of another man to God. Every man has a right to unblocked access to the source of spiritual reality.

In all these things democracy means for every individual that the essentials of a good life, mental, and moral, and spiritual, and physical are brought within reach. Human beings must not be asked to live on an inhuman level.

In every individual the possession of certain possibilities and powers leads to the possession of certain rights. And the deeper basis of these rights lies in the fact that as Paul said in his great sermon at Athens, "men are the offspring of God. As God's children they are God's sons in the making." Of course any man can say "no" to God. And here is the deepest tragedy of human life. And he can say "yes" to God. And here is the greatest glory of humanity. The divine word "All souls are mine," gives infinite promise to every individual who will receive the grace of God and set about following the divine will. God's care for every human being is not only the basis of democracy, it is the transfiguration of democracy. The dignity of man is the glory of God.

MANAGEMENT, LABOR, AGRICULTURE

HOW SHALL WE DEAL WITH LABOR UNION MONOPOLIES? [1]

DONALD RANDALL RICHBERG [2]

Donald Richberg gave this address before the Economic Club of Detroit, Michigan, on September 26, 1955.

The immediate background was obviously the negotiations then under way by the automobile workers' union for a "guaranteed annual wage" and the prospective consolidation of the American Federation of Labor and Congress of Industrial Organizations. (See George Meany, "The Principles and Program of AFL-CIO," below.)

Mr. Richberg was for years "on the side of labor." In this address, as he referred to his earlier leadership as a New Dealer and defender of labor, he appealed with unique authority to his "economic" audience of 1955.

His argument here, in line with his long legal thinking and experience, was heavily buttressed with legal citations and cases and well-organized development of his thesis, i.e., the rise of labor union monopolies and how to control them.

What, he asked, are the results of the labor monopoly? He cited the use of "fraud, coercion, violence" practiced by labor organizations through strikes. "As collective bargaining has grown so one-sided as now to be collective coercion, labor unions insist on retaining and using the supplemental weapon of personal violence to enforce their demands." He denounced the "wholesale and willful violations of criminal law" and the practice of the compulsory closed shop.

Mr. Richberg's solution was to extend the prohibition of compulsory unionism by both Federal and state laws. He would have "definite limitation of the exemption of the labor unions" in the application and enforcement of antitrust acts. He called for legislation relating to more constructive interpretation of the Clayton Act and the Norris-LaGuardia Act. And behind such legislative acts must be the development of a public opinion more alert to the problem of growing labor monopolies and their exercise of quasi-legal and downright illegal power.

Thus the speech clearly drew the lines of labor monopolies vs. public interest. As the years ahead mark bigger "bigness" in corporations and

[1] Text and permission for this reprint through the courtesy of Donald R. Richberg.

[2] For biographical note, see Appendix.

corresponding bigness of labor organizations, the issues are clear: Shall American centralized government be unduly dominated by either of these rival interests? Shall American versions of fascism, nazism, or other economic-political ideologies emerge? Or shall the balanced interests of popular American government continue? Congressional and state legislature debates will more and more grapple with this basic issue.

To forestall an indignant unionist question: What do you mean by "labor union monopolies?" let me begin with two assurances:

First. I am not charging organized labor with any intentions or designs not openly asserted by the outstanding leaders of organized labor.

Second. I am not charging these leaders with any greater wickedness than the inevitable ambition of human beings to expand autocratic powers so that they become destructive of the essential liberties of other people.

To prove my first point, I need only quote again the official declaration of the American Federation of Labor in the Supreme Court of the United States that "workers cannot thrive, but can only die under competition between themselves," and that their freedom of organization "must comprehend the right to eliminate wage competition between individual employees." In addition to this long-standing and oft repeated declaration, it is evident, in the prevailing demand for merger or close collaboration between all unions, that labor leaders are seeking also to eliminate all competition between unions, except their inevitable competition to obtain and retain as many members as possible.

To make my second point clear I hope, in my condemnation of labor union practices, to preserve the sense of humor with which I received at one time the private explanation of John L. Lewis that, when he publicly denounced me as "a renegade from labor who had turned against the breast that had suckled him," there was "nothing personal" in his critical statement.

The first thing to be made plain today is how organized labor has been advancing from a highly competitive force in a system of private enterprise into the position of a monopolistic controller of a more and more socialized economy.

Those who have studied, or have long memories, know that when the Sherman law passed in 1890 there was a rapidly growing fear among the American people that increasing business combinations and concentrations of economic power were threatening us with a controlled economy. This would not be a socialistic state, but something more in the nature of a corporative or Fascist state in which the control of industry would rest largely in the managers of giant businesses which, through their economic power, would render popular government submissive to their directions.

It was somewhat of a shock, particularly to organized labor, that in our early experience under the Sherman law its restraints were held applicable to ordinary and not unreasonable activities of the unions. As a result, with the support of a friendly public opinion, the Clayton Act was passed in 1914, definitely providing for an exemption of labor organizations from prosecution under the Sherman law when lawfully carrying out their legitimate objects. The labor organizations themselves were not to be construed as illegal conspiracies in restraint of trade.

However, the decisions of the Supreme Court in the 1920's held this exemption of labor unions to be so limited that further agitation arose against what was regarded as an increasing abuse of the injunctive powers of the Federal courts. This resulted in the passage of the Norris-LaGuardia Act which extended the definition of a labor dispute to cover a wide range of controversies. It then restricted the issuance of injunctions so as to make it difficult for the Federal courts to exercise much judicial control over union activities, particularly in strikes.

The judicial pendulum then swung strongly toward the labor side until today, under decisions of the Supreme Court, there is a practical exemption of labor unions from prosecution in the Federal courts for monopolistic practices, including the lawless carrying on of what are clearly illegitimate objects of labor organization.

One case in the Supreme Court should make the situation clear without resorting to extensive legalistic arguments.

The origin of this case lay in the action of the electrical workers' union in establishing, by a series of contracts with business managers, a practical monopoly in the supply of electrical equipment in New York City. There is no doubt as to what was accomplished because, when the case came to the Supreme Court (*Allen Bradley Co.* v. *Local Union No. 3*) . . . the opinion of the Court defined the agreement as follows: "It intended to and did restrain trade and monopolize the supply of electrical equipment in the New York City area to the exclusion of equipment manufactured in and shipped in from other states, and did also control its price and discriminate between its would-be customers." Then the Court said: "Our problem in this case is therefore a very narrow one—do labor unions violate the Sherman Act when, in order to further their own interests as wage earners, they aid and abet businessmen to do the precise things which that Act prohibits?"

The Court then observed that Congress did not intend to give labor unions the power to destroy a competitive economy and asserted very vigorously: "Seldom, if ever, has it been claimed before, that by permitting labor unions to carry on their own activities, Congress intended completely to abdicate its constitutional power to regulate interstate commerce and to empower interested business groups to shift our society from a competitive to a monopolistic economy."

The Court acknowledged the inconsistency in a law which provided that labor unions alone could destroy competition, but not in combination with business groups, and then held: "This, it is argued, brings about a wholly undesirable result— one which leaves labor unions free to engage in conduct which restrains trade. But the desirability of such an exemption of labor unions is a question for the determination of Congress."

The curious final ruling of the Supreme Court in this case was to the effect that a labor union and a group of employers could not amicably make such a monopolistic agreement as was effective in New York City. But when a union proceeded one by one against employers and, by use of its so-called economic power, compelled employers one by one to make monopolistic agreements, this inevitable restraint of trade would be beyond the power of the Federal courts to prevent by invocation of the Sherman Act.

It should be stated that, in the series of Supreme Court opinions which have resulted in the sanctioning of the exercise of monopolistic powers by labor unions, there have been vigorous dissents, the late Chief Justice Hughes having been one of the notable dissenters. So there may be a just criticism of the Supreme Court majority whose opinions have been largely responsible for permitting labor unions by lawless activities for illegitimate objects to extend a monopoly power wider and wider in American industry.

It seems to me the Supreme Court is particularly to be criticized for such a decision as in the Apex case . . . where the dissenting opinion of Chief Justice Hughes pointed out that the evidence disclosed "a sit-down strike in its most aggravated and illegal form," and where he summarized the lawless activities of the union as follows:

When the Union demanded a closed shop agreement and, on its refusal, declared the strike, only eight of the Company's twenty-five hundred employees were members of the Union. The Company's plant was seized and held for several weeks. Its machinery and equipment were 'wantonly demolished or damaged to the extent of many thousands of dollars.'

There was not merely a stoppage of production, but there was also a deliberate prevention of the shipment of finished goods to customers outside the state."

It might seem clear to a straight thinking citizen that, when a law explicitly exempted from its prosecution only the "lawful" activities of an organization in carrying out its "legitimate objects," the exemption could not be legally extended to protect the violent lawlessness of a union representing only eight of twenty-five hundred employees which sought to compel an employer to make a closed shop agreement, forcing all his employees to join the union or lose their jobs.

You will not be bored with any repetition of the tortuous reasoning by which the Supreme Court has rewritten and expanded the statute law. But it may be appropriate for me to quote the reply of the late Chief Justice Taft when I heard an eminent lawyer argue before him that the Court simply could not construe a statute to read as the Court had apparently construed it. The amiable Chief Justice jocularly said: "Mr. B., I think you underestimate the powers of the Supreme Court." Unfortunately for many lawyers and for the good of the country, it is becoming more and more difficult every year to underestimate the powers of the Supreme Court.

Now we come to the crucial question: How shall we deal with labor union monopolies? There is no doubt of their existence. We have today something like seventeen million wage earners organized in unions of enormous size and power. These unions are entrenched in the economic power which goes with the ability to paralyze a single plant or an entire industry by merely a concerted refusal to work. In addition, these unions, by their numbers of voters allied in self-interest and organized for political action, are able to obtain favoring legislation and administration and to prevent even mild limitations upon their exercise of dictatorial powers.

These unions are able to pursue their objectives, not only by lawful methods in peacefully and concertedly stopping work, but also by the use of lawless force and violence, unchecked by judicial or executive enforcement of the criminal laws. These laws protect life and property against all kinds of fraud, coercion and violence except those practiced by labor organizations for the unlawful purpose of preventing men from obtaining employment by employers who want to employ them.

Many years ago, when I was legal adviser to a large number of labor organizations, I undertook to protest to the head of one, who was a genial, humane person, against the use of violent tactics which I felt he could more effectively discourage. He did not like what was going on, particularly as his union was not very strong and public opinion was being alienated. But he said to me with a sigh: "Don, a strike ain't no pink tea."

Let us be candid with one another about this. A strike is never a pink tea. As a matter of fact, a strike is a great hardship to most of the men who engage in it. In a long strike they are bound to lose more than the value of anything they may personally gain. They must be emotionally aroused to feel that they are fighting through necessity for what they ought to have. Under such emotion men are not inclined to be reasonable or peaceful. They don't need much encouragement to be individ- ually lawless; and, in mass picketing and such concerted action, they will incline to sadistic cruelty.

This is not the time and place to discuss in detail antistrike legislation. But it is appropriate to say that, to check the grow- ing monopoly power of organized labor, it would be wise to write national and state laws to insure the enforcement of the ordinary criminal laws in labor disputes, just as they are en- forced in all other conflicts of human interest.

This might not end the venality or political timidity of local officials who won't enforce the law against union labor. But if there were adequate national and state laws to forbid and pre- vent labor violence there would always be at least the possibility of imposing direct responsibility for keeping the peace upon the governor of a state and upon the President of the United States. Behind them stand the armed forces of the states and the nation. It is the duty of these forces to preserve the people of the United States and their liberties not only from foreign aggression, but also from domestic violence and anarchy.

There was once hope that, when the labor organizations obtained greater strength in numbers and better legal protection for their legitimate activities, they would cease to use organized violence to accomplish their ends. It was the belief of many frinds of labor, such as myself, that the legal and economic dis- advantages of the unions furnished excuses for criminal conduct which would disappear when a genuine balance of economic power made collective bargaining a two-sided business. Un- fortunately, we have seen, as collective bargaining has grown so one-sided as now to be collective coercion, labor unions insist on retaining and using the supplemental weapon of personal violence to enforce their demands.

Without disregarding a long line of extensive and vicious uses of criminal force, let me refer to three recent examples, no one of which carried with it any possible justification for the crimes with which union demands were supported.

In a strike against the Southern Telephone Company, property was damaged extensively and individuals assaulted with a recklessness and frequency which made absurd the protests of union officials that they did not condone such wrongdoing.

In a strike against the Louisville-Nashville Railroad, bridges were dynamited and burned, individuals were assaulted and homes terrorized, in aid of a strike maintained by the so-called conservative railway unions.

In a long strike against the Kohler Company in Wisconsin, the CIO people have been guilty of every sort of terrorism, resulting in the death of at least one man, wholesale injuries to others, and much destruction of property. In addition, city authorities have been so intimidated that it has been impossible to deliver supplies needed by the Kohler Company not only through Sheboygan, but also through the large port of Milwaukee, Wisconsin.

It seems incredible, in a country where men are sent to jail constantly for street fighting, or stealing, or destroying property, that great, so-called "respectable" organizations of labor are permitted to carry forward openly campaigns of violence and terrorism to support themselves in exercising an economic power which, even without accompanying violence, is so great as to make collective bargaining almost a mockery.

Turning aside from the obvious need to prevent labor unions from increasing their monopoly power through wholesale and willful violations of the criminal law, let me call attention to two urgent needs for legal action to restrain this growing despotic power. First, is a legal restraint on compulsory unionism. Second, is a clear, enforceable limitation on the exemption of the unions from the Sherman antitrust law.

Compulsory unionism is an evil which has grown into vast size and consequence in recent years. In earlier times there was some defense under some circumstances for a union demand for a closed shop. Unions were struggling under legal handicaps and against an employer bargaining power which heavily outweighed their own. It was not unreasonable for a union, having obtained recognition and a contract with an employer, to wish to insure itself against immediate competition with nonunionists. It was not unreasonable for an employer sometimes to feel that he would have better relations with an entirely unionized force, and would have protection against competing unions or minority factions, if he made a closed shop contract with the prevailing labor managers.

But as the unions grew in size and extended their bargaining from single employers to regional groups and ultimately to all the substantial employers in an industry, the establishment of a union closed shop began to invest a strong union with entirely too much coercive power over, not only a regional group of employers, but over an entire industry. Thus, as we moved into the era of national strikes, with the paralysis of entire industries doing infinite harm, it became evident that the closed shop was such a menace that it could no longer be tolerated.

In this situation arose the pretense of a compromise with sound principle in the acceptance of what is called the union shop. The only good feature of the union shop is that an employer is permitted to seek employees outside of the ranks of union members. But the vital wrong in the union shop is that under such a contract every employee must, willy-nilly, become and remain a member of the union after he is employed. This means that countless liberty-loving persons who for one reason or another do not want to join a union are compelled to do so in order to earn a living.

The stock union argument, that the union represents all the employees, works for their benefit and should be supported by them, is a travesty upon individual liberty. The unions impose upon their members, by dues and assessments and otherwise, a host of obligations to support the union policies and activities which go far beyond the narrow field of bargaining over wages and working conditions.

The unions have become the political spokesmen for their members, and, despite minor legal limitations, they are able to use the funds contributed by their members to support public policies, social and political programs and propaganda, with which a large part of their membership may entirely disagree.

It is an outrage that an American citizen should be compelled to be a member of a political organization to whose policies and programs he is opposed. It is an outrage that a free American should be compelled to join and to support and to submit to the discipline of any private organization to which he does not wish to belong. The United States Constitution and the constitutions of all the states carry with them guarantees of civil rights which are flagrantly violated by compulsory unionism.

There are today eighteen states which forbid all forms of compulsory unionism. Although the union shop contract is tolerated in the Taft-Hartley Act, there is a saving clause permitting the enforcement of these contrary state laws.

One of the major drives of the unions today is to repeal and to stop the extension of these state laws. It should be a vital part of the political thinking of all American citizens to extend the prohibition of compulsory unionism in both Federal and state laws. This is one method of dealing with the growing labor union monopoly which is obvious and practical.

Heretofore I explained how the improper exemption of labor organizations from prosecutions under the antitrust acts has grown. The remedy for this evil is clearly that pointed out in the Supreme Court opinion to which I referred. A definite limitation of the exemption of the labor unions should be enacted by Congress.

All that is necessary is to write in plain terms a new definition of what the Federal law means in exempting labor unions from the antitrust acts when "lawfully carrying out the legitimate objects" thereof.

If I had the drafting of such a law, I should define the word "lawfully" to include only peaceful, orderly activities, but not "any uses of fraud, force, violence or intimidation or any conspiracy to violate or to prevent enforcement of any law of the United States or of one of the several states."

In addition, in order to release the shackles placed on the Federal courts by Federal statutes as interpreted by the Supreme Court, there should be a provision in the law that nothing in the Clayton Act or the Norris-La Guardia Act should restrict the jurisdiction of a Federal court to issue an injunction against a labor organization, or its members or supporters, against conduct which is found to be not "lawfully carrying out the legitimate objects" of such an organization.

Of course nothing which has been suggested in the way of dealing with the growing labor union monopolies can be made effective except through political action which must be based on a widespread reappraisal of the social value of and the public service rendered by labor unions.

There has grown up in this country an enormous body of public opinion which, despite their many abuses of power, always comes to the support of labor unions in critical conflicts. These unions are rightly regarded as institutions which *can* be fostered to serve worthy purposes. But there have been terrifying revelations in thousands of pages of testimony regarding the evils perpetrated by many unions under criminal, subversive or reckless leadership. Certainly no one can read these official records of organized crime, extortion and disloyalty without realizing that legal prevention and restraint of the growth and inevitable abuse of such private powers are urgently needed.

The leaders of organized labor are ambitious human beings. They will not voluntarily abandon powers of public influence and private profit that grow greater every day. They will continue to expand their powers until their abuse and their menace to the public welfare become so great that something in the nature of a revolutionary struggle will be necessary to relieve the American people from the domination of the latest autocracy which threatens internally to destroy our constitutional form of government and our constitutional liberties.

It would be far better for the American people to begin today to take away from the labor unions the special privileges and despotic powers which are undermining our industrial health, while this can still be done without a conflict approaching the intensity and cruelty of a civil war. Such a political struggle would be a bitter battle, but one which would greatly serve the American people to reduce the menace of foreign aggression as well as to halt the spread of intolerable domestic lawlessness.

THE PRINCIPLES AND PROGRAM OF AFL-CIO [3]

GEORGE MEANY [4]

President George Meany gave this address on Monday, December 5, 1955, before the merged American Federation of Labor and the Congress of Industrial Organizations, in the Seventy-first Regiment Armory at Thirty-fourth Street and Madison Avenue, New York City.

The occasion was the first convention of these combined unions. The AFL-CIO brought together after a twenty-year split the AFL with some ten million members and 109 unions and the CIO with some five million members and thirty-two unions. Some 1,400 delegates and 4,500 guests and reporters composed the immediate audience. Mr Meany became the first president. Walter Reuther was elected head of the subdivision, the Industrial Union Department, with sixty-six unions, organized on factory-wide as contrasted with craft basis membership.

President Eisenhower, from his home in Gettysburg, Pennsylvania, gave a seven-minute talk by telephone to the audience. His voice was clear and strong. At the end the crowded audience of perhaps five thousand rose and applauded.

Mr. Meany, in his speech of acceptance, took as his premise, "all our actions must be keyed to that simple, plain principle that a trade union has no other reason for existence than the job of carrying forward and advancing the interests and welfare of its members." Throughout the speech he attempted to sound the note of labor's unanimity of purpose and method. Thus he indicated or implied, as had Samuel Gompers years ago, as president of the AFL, that labor, although always having a decisive stake and policy in legislative and governmental programs, should not set itself up as a labor political party. He reminded the listeners that the common front of labor should be in their constant program of economic betterment; their adherence to the principles of constitutional government (as against the overriding of Supreme Court decisions by "white supremacy advocates"); their resistance to Communistic infiltrations; and their support of those economic and political activities that would help this country to support the cause of "human liberty everywhere" and to carry on successfully the "cold war." He was especially vigorous and bitter in denouncing the Soviet's foreign policy and warned against occasional businessmen and politicians who might fall for this "Communist propaganda." The climax of his address had to do significantly with the disavowal of "any sentiment for labor to take over one the existing parties."

[3] Text supplied by the American Federation of Labor and reprinted here through the courtesy of President George Meany.

[4] For biographical note, see Appendix.

In general, the address was well balanced in its analysis of these issues, economic, social, political, and international, and augured well for the stable future of semiconservative unionism with its enlarged sphere of influence and responsibility.

Mr. Meany, prior to this convention speech and later, gave other addresses that supplemented the topics briefly handled before his December 5 audience. And those speeches, more than this general one, registered more impressively and persuasively his mature judgments and reasoning on the fundamentals of labor's philosophy at mid-century. He was always well armed with facts, solid in his reasoning, not inclined, as was John L. Lewis at times, to resort to abstract eloquence. President Meany on December 9 addressed the National Manufacturers Association in its annual session at the Waldorf-Astoria. His was a notably conservative and conciliatory speech.

General sentiment throughout the nation, in view of the merger and President Meany's speech of acceptance, seemed to accept the consolidation as a trend in American bigness, but questioned whether or not danger lay in the vast power conferred. Organized labor, most believed, had achieved for the first time relative security and therefore would be less likely to break out with rash or irresponsible acts.

Mr. Meany grew up in the Bronx, New York City. He left high school in his second year and soon after became a member of the plumbers' union. But he read much and had unusual retentiveness. Also he was a natural-born speaker. He talked often in the Wednesday night meetings of his union and soon demonstrated leadership as organizer, debater, and dominating speaker. He rose rapidly in unionism and in 1939 was elected to the national AFL office in Washington, from which he emerged as national president. He was chiefly responsible for the union of the two major organizations.[6]

Chairman Harry Bates: And I declare George Meany duly elected as President of the American Federation of Labor and the Congress of Industrial Organizations for the ensuing term.

President Meany, I deem it a great honor and privilege to present to you this gavel. I know that you will conduct the affairs of this great organization with credit and honor to yourself and to the interests of the 15 million members of the organization, and to the country as a whole. I wish you every success in your future endeavors.

Mr. Meany: President Reuther, representatives of the former organizations which have joined here today, the Executive Board

[6] For further comment on George Meany as speaker, see *Representative American Speeches: 1953-54,* p43-9.

of the CIO, Executive Council of the American Federation of Labor, and delegates in attendance at this most important convention:

I feel that this is the most important trade union development of our time. Whether we deserve the attention or not, I am quite sure that surely the eyes of workers all over the world are on this meeting this morning. Millions of workers, millions of ordinary people behind the Iron Curtain of despotism and degradation are looking towards us this morning with eyes of hope. Many millions more who live in the shadow of that curtain of inequity are, I am sure, praying for the success of this organization which we are bringing into being today.

I can readily understand the feeling of elation which I sense present here today among the delegates and surely among the officers over the end of these years of division and of the inauguration of this new united movement. I, too, share that feeling of elation that we have come this far along the road to unity for all labor in America. But when I think of the opportunities that lie ahead and of the tremendous responsibilities that go with those opportunities I give way to some sober thoughts as to our obligation to meet the test, not only of grasping these opportunities for moving forward, but also of removing the obstacles and solving the problems that will lie in our path of meeting the test of great responsibility that goes with an organization of 15 million citizens in a nation of 160 million people.

I think in approaching this task we should take a serious and good look at ourselves to make sure that we know just what our obligations are and to make sure that we have the type of organization that can meet these obstacles and grasp these opportunities to better the day both in the life and work of the great mass of the workers of this nation. We must think in terms of the true meaning of a trade union movement, a movement that has for its sole, definite and single purpose the advancement of the welfare and interest of the great mass of workers who are part of this movement.

That must be the motivating influence and manner in which we move forward. Let all of our actions be keyed into that simple, plain principle that a trade union has no other reason for existence than the job of carrying out and carrying forward and advancing the interests and welfare of its members.

In building and advancing the cause of our union let us not think in terms of personal prestige, of having a big union for the sake of having a big union. Let us not think in terms of a great big financial structure and of great power. Let us think in terms of the simple philosophy of those who founded this movement of advancing the cause of workers.

As we go forward together in this movement, let us stop thinking in terms of prior labels. Let us make up our minds that from this moment on there is just one label on all the organizations and all of the membership of this great organization, and that label is AFL-CIO and nothing else. Let us apply this philosophy in terms of good faith, determination to live together, to work together, and to think together for one united organization.

We have brought into being this morning a trade union instrumentality to carry out the work we have all been engaged in and to do it a little better, we feel, than we were able to do it as a divided movement. We have a Constitution that we worked on for many, many long weeks. We make no claim as to its perfection, but we do feel that it is an instrument under which we can live and that it carries with it the principles that we have always had in this movement in this country of complete and absolute autonomy for each and every organization to run its own affairs. It contains the voluntary principle upon which our movement was founded in the early days.

It was once said many years ago that that government is best which governs least. It is in that spirit that we wrote this constitution. After all, we are practical enough to realize that the words in the constitution would not have very much meaning if we did not enter into the work of this organization in a spirit of mutual respect, in a spirit of cooperation and in a spirit dedicated to the principle that unions are created for the benefit of the workers who toil for wages.

We must grow, this trade union movement, with the nation, but we must grow in a right way. Let us organize the unorganized. Let us not waste our time and our efforts trying to reorganize those who are already organized.

Let us try to bring the blessings and benefits that we know are inherent in a trade union movement to the millions of those who are still unorganized. Then as we face the future this morning where there is a great spirit, as I said before, of elation and happiness, we should give some sober thought to the kind of world that we live in, to the problems that we have at home and the problems that we have abroad, to the problems that we face in the new industrial age which is coming upon us, to the problems that have been ever present in the conduct of the relations of our country with the other nations of the world.

Let us understand that despite the many advances, despite the great achievements of the organized labor movement over the years, we still have those who believe that we would be better off without unions; those who believe in the archaic traditions of the 1880's and 1890's; those who believe that America is built from the top down, that if you keep the great corporations fat and wealthy enough will trickle down to keep those at the lower level of our economic structure happy and contented. We still have this opposition, and this opposition has made its mark in the last seven or eight years.

We would be less than truthful if we did not admit to ourselves that the legislative trend in so far as liberal and remedial legislation is concerned, legislation in which we have a vital interest, that legislative trend in the last eight years has been backward and not forward. And it is up to us, using every weapon that we have at our command under the Constitution of this country, using every method that is legal to advance the cause of the workers. It is up to us to reverse that trend.

We have come a long way in building up the standard of life and of work with the people of this great nation, but we can't say that we have come all the way. We can't afford to look back for any other reason except to draw from the experiences of the past in order to apply their lessons to move forward for the future. We have no right to look back with a feeling of satisfaction, because there is still much to be done. We still need better schools and more schools for the children of

America. We hear from time to time the great orators of our political parties, especially during the season of the year when the schools are graduating their children, about America's greatest possession, the future of America, the children of America. And we are still in the disgraceful position where we cannot say that we have adequate facilities to train and educate those children. And we have got to wipe out this idea; that this is the job of each and every little community, no matter what its economic or financial position might be. If the children of America are the nation's wealth of the future, if they are our most proud possession, then they are the concern of the entire nation, and the nation itself should take a hand through Federal aid to education to see that we have good schools.

Then we have housing. That is still a problem. Yes, we have made some forward strides, but we still have a long way to go. We still have thousands and thousands and tens of thousands of people who are living in slums, who have not as yet received the full benefits of which we like to boast, of the great and high standard of life that we have here in our American continent.

We need better roads. We need to improve our social security system. We need to bring about a system of medical care that will take care of the health of the nation as a whole. These problems must be met.

Then we have the problem that strikes right home, the problem of preserving the right of workers to improve their conditions through the instrumentality of a trade union, the problem of seeing to it that the labor-management act on our statute books is made fair to both labor and management, and not an instrument by which management, if it will, can destroy or hamper the development of trade unions.

We have got to amend that Act and we have got to wipe off the statute books of eighteen states the so-called right-to-work laws which are laws destructive of the rights of union workers.

Then we must think soberly of our position as a nation and of the things we like to feel are really in the tradition of America. We speak of our freedom, we speak of the Founding Fathers. We speak of the Constitution and the Bill of Rights.

I think we have some right to be proud of those things, to be proud of our tradition and our heritage; but I think we have no right to complacently sit by as long as those rights are denied to any portion of the population of this great country.

We have had striking evidence in the last few days, if we needed any such evidence, that the Constitution of the United States and the Bill of Rights and the civil liberties that we all like to boast of do not prevail in certain parts of our country for people whose skin is a little different in color than that of ourselves. We have men who call themselves statesmen who are public servants, elected by the people, and still who, in the interest of white supremacy, defy a decision of the United States Supreme Court in regard to desegregation. Yes, they are amending the Constitution to suit themselves insofar as its application is concerned, and what they are saying in effect is that this Constitution does not prevail in the Southland.

I say to these people, a good many of whom call themselves Christians, that when they go to church on Sunday they should remember that the words "and thy neighbor as thyself" are still an integral part of the Ten Commandments, and they should apply that in dealing with their fellow men.

Then we have got to give some sober thought today to our duties as citizens, taking our place in the community life of the nation, making our contribution to good government, making our contribution as citizens to the policies of our Government in dealing with other nations of the world.

In my book labor not only has a right to raise its voice in regard to the policies under which our Federal Government is administered, but we have a duty as citizens to take part in shaping the policies of our Government; and as workers we have a special interest in the foreign policy of our Government. We have a special interest in seeing to it that our Government makes its full contribution to the preservation of human freedom everywhere on this earth where it is possible to make a contribution.

A free trade union requires an atmosphere of freedom, and we have long ago learned in this shrinking world of ours that the enslavement of workers anywhere, the denial of the right of workers to have free trade unions anywhere, is a threat to free labor everywhere, which includes the United States of America. And we know where the major threat comes to world freedom. We don't have to be diplomatic in analyzing this question. We don't have to deceive ourselves. We can call the shots as we see them. We have no commercial, political or financial reason to see peace where there is no peace. We have been meeting this cold war situation for many years, beginning with the Truman Plan in 1946, the Marshall Plan, the NATO, Point Four, and everything else, and I think up until this spring meeting it quite successfully.

Then of course we run into the new "smiling face" technique of those who would destroy us and destroy every right that we hold dear. At the conclusion of the Summit Conference in July we were told that it was a great success, that the spirit of Geneva had lessened tensions and everything was going to be fine. We were told that by the heads of our Government. I say to you here today that when we were told that the American people were hoodwinked. It was not a success; I wish to God it was.

The American people were fooled, if you please, and told that tensions were lessened, and everything was going to be all right. We were told that we should now shake the hands of these who would deny us our freedom, these who would destroy us. We were told that tensions would be lessened.

Well, I can say personally I have searched with painstaking care for these lessened tensions. What do I find in that search? I find the same old line, a new threat in the blockade of Berlin, attempting to throw those people into the Godless ideology of Communism by saying that East Berlin is no longer under the Four-Power rule, that it is under the rule of their so-called satellite state, the so-called East German democratic government.

As a contribution to these lessened tensions we see Egypt armed by a Communist satellite for attack. Then we see the tour of slander, where the top people representing the Soviet Union are using India as a sounding board for their attacks upon the free nations of the world.

Then we see the foreign ministers' conference five weeks ago, which was supposed to carry out and implement the agreements reached at Geneva in July. There we see a complete repudiation of everything that was done at the July high level conference.

Then we see the stepped-up war preparations of Moscow's partner in the Far East.

Let me give you an idea of the people we are told to extend the hand of fellowship to—an idea of their philosophy—the . . . [head] of Moscow's Far East branch, Mao Tse-tung. In a manual distributed to his people a few months ago he had this to say:

> Our war is sacred, just and progressive and aims at peace. We aim at peace not only in one country but also throughout the world, and we not only aim at temporary peace but at a permanent peace. In order to achieve this objective, we must wage a life and death struggle until our aim is achieved.

That is the philosophy of Moscow's Far East partners who are now stepping up preparations for war on their neighbors.

Then we see the increased pressure on the Adenauer government. We have seen in the last week or so the H-bomb blast in the Gobi desert. Then just to show that they are just the same at home in applying their ideology we had a new purge where some of the top men, assistants to Beria, were put up against the wall and destroyed.

This, then, is the spirit of Geneva. This is the thing that came out of Geneva in July, the child of American faith and Soviet fraud. We have got to think of this thing because we know that the kind of instrumentality we are creating here today cannot and will not exist unless it exists in an atmosphere of freedom and under a system of government such as we have. The businessman, perhaps, can afford to fall for this Communist propaganda, and of course politicians from time to time see peace and progress in these negotiations where there is no peace and no progress.

Labor has never been neutral in its relations with dictatorship or tyranny. We were never non-Nazi when Hitler was

riding high. We were not non-Fascists in the days of Mus-
solini; we were anti-Fascists. And we are also not non-Falangists
in regard to Franco Spain; we are anti-Falangists. We can't
afford the luxury in these trying days of being non-Communist
or neutral; we are not; and we must and shall be anti-Communist.

In meeting all these problems at home and abroad we must
be mindful of our duty to the nation as a whole, because as it
was well said here a few minutes ago, what is good for the
nation is good for us. We have got to show the American
people that this movement, this organization is dedicated to the
good of our nation, to the good of all the citizens of our nation.
Who can deny that higher wages and better working conditions
are not good for America? Who can deny that the purchasing
power built up largely through the instrumentality of free trade
unions is not the most vital factor in this dynamic economy of
ours? Who can deny that trade unions are dedicated to the
welfare of the nation as a whole? Yes, we are going to use
every means at our disposal to carry forth our program both at
home and abroad. We are going to continue to support the
International Confederation of Free Trade Unions in its fight to
keep labor free and in due time to strike the chains from those
who are enslaved behind the Iron Curtain.

We are going to use our economic weapon in dealing with
the employers, if that is necessary, in order to get a fair share of
the wealth that we jointly produce with management. And we
are going to meet those who would destroy our movement and
who would turn back the clock—we are going to meet them on
the political front, if you please.

I am somewhat amused by this hue and cry about labor
political activity, about the labor bosses controlling votes. I am
sure they know that we don't control votes. No one—no one
can tell the American worker how he has got to vote, and that
includes you, me and everybody else.

I sometimes wonder about these people who are making
these statements about labor political power. I am wondering
if their consciences are starting to bother them. What is our
political philosophy? Our political philosophy is to inform our

own people on the issue that they have before them, and in particular to the issues that affect the welfare of our own people.

Are the members of the United States Senate opposed to an intelligent electorate? I thought when they run for office—and I have heard many of them—I thought they all said that they wanted the public to always be informed; they wanted them to know about these issues. Well, that is what we want. We want our people to be informed on all the issues facing the electorate, and we want in particular for them to be informed on the issues that affect their lives and their daily work.

They are worried now about a labor party. Well, I don't see any sentiment for a labor party, and I don't see any sentiment for labor to take over one of the existing parties. That is a new one now, that we are going to take over one of the existing parties. Well, I know this, that we have a right and a duty to meet those who are opposed to us wherever they present the challenge.

In the early days we met the starvation method. We met the company thug, the company spy, the company injunction and the company judge. We met the American plan, so-called, designed to destroy our movement. And now where is the challenge? The challenge is in the legislative halls, and our answer is political education, and political activity, because if we are going to carry on this work they have proved beyond question that they can hamstring us and render us impotent by adverse legislation. And if we are going to carry on this work as we must, we must meet that challenge in the legislative halls, and that means political education.

As I said before, in carrying out our work we must do so in a way that will commend us to our neighbor. After all, the American worker is just a part, one part, one segment of this great, big family we call the United States of America; a big segment, if you please, but still a segment.

We must carry on our work in a way that will bring commendation from those with whom we come in contact. We must try to conduct our affairs in consonance with the high principles upon which our movement is founded and which we are attempting to carry forward. I feel this we can do.

For myself, I appreciate beyond question, beyond doubt, beyond means to express to you the confidence that you have shown, that my colleagues of the AFL and CIO have shown in entrusting to me this very responsible task. I will give myself to it as best I can. I am not given to predictions. I tell you now I will never surrender principle for expediency. I tell you now that, in so far as it is my place to influence decisions, those decisions will be made without regard to where the union formerly was and without regard to how big or how little a union is.

Let us remember that on this very, very happy occasion we have merely taken the first step, that we have created a tool, an instrumentality, something that we can use to carry forward for the people we represent; and if we carry forward in good faith in our relations with one another and true to the principles and traditions upon which our movement was founded, I am sure that we can succeed.

So let us face the future, confident beyond question that the cause we espouse, confident beyond expression that the things we ask for are just and proper. And if we do this—and I am sure that we will—then with God's help we shall not fail.

FARM SURPLUSES AND THE SOIL BANK [6]

EZRA TAFT BENSON [7]

Ezra Taft Benson, Secretary of Agriculture, United States Department of Agriculture, gave this address before the American National Cattlemen's Association, at New Orleans, Louisiana, at eleven o'clock in the morning, January 10, 1956. On the preceding day, President Eisenhower had presented to Congress his special farm message. The President had recommended a "soil bank" as the key feature of a nine-point program for ending a five-year decline in farm economy. Mr. Benson's address was a summary and defense of the principal recommendations of that message.

Secretary Benson, generally regarded as a well-balanced, highly experienced authority on farm problems, had nevertheless been continually criticized by farmers, Democrats, and many Republicans since his appointment in January 1953. He was held responsible for the Administration's failure to solve the problem of farm surpluses and declining farm prices. He had stalwartly pursued his policy of "flexible supports," and repeatedly affirmed, as he had done as early as 1943, that "the virus of subsidies permeates the economic body and eats it up once it gets its proboscis under the skin." In attempts to inform this nation of the complicated problems and the many factors of solution, he had spoken up and down the land before all kinds of organizations, had taken to the air, and expounded to congressional committees. During these three years he had talked with indefatigable zeal and with much speaking effectiveness. His speeches were logically developed, clearly stated, although with some detachment that failed to persuade his critics. He buttressed his reasoning with concrete data that repeatedly refuted his opponents. His delivery was vehement but more academic than rabble rousing. His large physical size and confident manner added to his platform leadership. Behind his speeches were his deep religious convictions, the ring of sincerity. He disavowed partisanship and spoke out frankly to all inquirers and critics.

On the day following this New Orleans address, Secretary Benson appeared for three hours before the Senate Agriculture Committee. He defended his stand on the soil bank only because "we're faced with a serious situation." Asked whether his testimony meant that the soil bank would create more problems he frankly declared, "Absolutely!"

---

[6] Text furnished with this permission for reprinting, through the courtesy of Mr. Ezra Taft Benson.

[7] For biographical note, see Appendix.

On January 18 Senator George D. Aiken, of Vermont, introduced a bill to implement the President's special farm message. A radically revised bill incorporating both the soil bank and rigid price supports was passed by Congress and vetoed by President Eisenhower on April 16. At the time of writing it appeared certain that the soil bank would be retained in whatever version of the farm bill was finally enacted.

I am highly honored indeed, and feel deeply my responsibilities in meeting with so many of you today—both you in this hall, and those I am privileged to reach by radio in their homes throughout the land.

Yesterday President Eisenhower sent to the Congress his special message on agriculture. It is the recommendations in that message that I wish principally to discuss with you today.

The program presented by the President is the Administration's program—it is my program—and it is your program because it came from the grass roots. We asked for—and we received—the suggestions and criticisms of literally thousands of farmers and ranchers, in every type of agriculture, from every part of the country. We worked closely with the bipartisan National Agricultural Advisory Commission. I thank all of you for your interest, and for the ideas you contributed. These recommendations represent valuable additions to our sound, basic program of 1954.

These are troubled times for families on our farms and ranches. Our nation has been blessed with unprecedented prosperity—but it is a prosperity in which families on the land have not adequately shared.

We must free the farm economy from the distortions that had their roots in wartime needs. The plain fact is that wartime production incentives were continued too long. We must provide means for cutting down surpluses. We must widen markets. We must help farmers and ranchers cut costs, balance production, and increase their incomes.

Farm people deserve their full share of this nation's prosperity. I did not become Secretary of Agriculture of the United States to stand idly by wringing my hands while our farm families suffer year after year of economic decline.

The nine-point program we propose is a workable approach. Here is what it will do: It will reduce surpluses. It will gradually bring production and markets into balance at fair prices. It will provide more economic security and a fairer share of the national income for farm people.

We are blessed in America as are few other people by the abundance with which our agriculture can produce. Yet the biggest difficulty we face in our farm problem is the mountainous surpluses that have accumulated—the results, I repeat, of wartime incentives too long continued.

Our economists estimate that farm prices right now might be as much as 10 per cent higher if we did not have these surpluses. Think of that!

They estimate that these surpluses reduced farm income by the staggering sum of more than $2 billion in 1955. Without these surpluses net farm income last year might have been as much as 20 per cent higher. Think of that!

Your Federal Government now has some $7.7 billion invested in price-support operations—including an inventory so huge that storage charges alone are about $1 million a day.

We have made tremendous efforts to dispose of these surpluses. During the past three years we have moved into consumption more than $4 billion worth of these surpluses. Yet for each bushel equivalent sold, about one and a half has replaced it in the stockpiles.

Nor is this all. As the President said in his message, "Other consequences of past farm programs have been no less damaging. Both at home and abroad, markets have been lost. Foreign farm production has been increased. American exports have declined. Foreign products have been attracted to our shores."

Shrinking markets, particularly for the crops we normally export in quantity, have forced drastic acreage controls upon our farmers. In the past two years, compelled by old laws, farmers have taken 29 million acres out of wheat and cotton.

But this has not solved our problems. It has merely spread them. The diverted acres have been shifted to other crops— and the consequences onto other producers—until now almost every farmer and rancher, regardless of the crop or the livestock he raises, is hurt.

More than half of the diverted acres have been shifted into oats, barley, and grain sorghums—the end product of which has been still more meat, milk, and eggs at a time when production was already high and rising.

The disastrous consequences of continuing too long the incentives established during the war was obvious long before this Administration took office. Three years ago work began immediately on what became the Agricultural Act of 1954. Although it did not embody all the recommendations then made, this was—and is—sound legislation, developed and passed with bipartisan support. It included the essential principle of price flexibility to help keep supplies of various commodities in balance. Yet for two reasons the Act of 1954 is inadequate to the challenge before us. First, it only began to take hold with the harvests of 1955. Still more important, its operation is smothered by the pressure of surplus stocks amassed under the old program.

To make any sound, long-time program work, the surplus stocks must first be reduced to manageable proportions. We cannot continue merely to shift acres from one crop to another, building new and larger surpluses. Neither can we let the problems of crops become millstones around the necks of livestock producers.

Remedies are needed now—this year. We must go forward —not back to old programs that have failed so completely to serve the best interests of farm families.

If the Congress acts without delay, this program of immediate and lasting benefit will quickly begin to make itself felt. In terms of dollars, this could be a program involving more than one billion dollars—*this year,* partly in the form of commodities which the government already owns. I do not mean to say that it represents that much of an increase in farm net income, but it could be, I repeat, a billion dollar plus program for 1956.

In our recommendations, we have given full consideration to the interests of livestock producers. Cattle and calves are the largest single source of cash farm income—and livestock and its products, taken together, bring in about 56 per cent of all farm income from marketings.

To meet the twin problems of surpluses and diverted acres— to bring supplies into better balance with what our markets can profitably absorb—the President has recommended a soil bank. It is a soil bank of two parts—one immediate and short range in effect, the other pointed toward longer-time adjustments.

One part of the soil bank proposal has been called an acreage reserve. It would be voluntary and temporary. It calls for a temporary cut in production of the crops now in greatest surplus. Through temporarily reduced production it would provide opportunity to work down accumulated surpluses to more normal levels.

We are recommending that the Congress consider a voluntary additional reduction in the acreage of certain crops which today are in serious surplus—wheat, cotton, corn, and rice.

The essence of the recommendation is that farmers will voluntarily reduce plantings below their acreage allotments. In return they will receive certificates equal to a specified percentage of their normal yield on the acres they withhold. The certificates will be negotiable so farmers can convert them to cash. They will be redeemable by the Commodity Credit Corporation either in cash or in actual commodity at a specified rate.

This rate will be set as an incentive level high enough to assure the success of the program.

Because his income will be protected in this manner, the farmer will contract neither to graze nor to harvest any other crop from acres he puts into this reserve.

For an individual farm the program would work this way: A farmer with an allotment of 100 acres of wheat might choose to plant only 80 acres and to put the other 20 acres into the acreage reserve. His base acreage allotment would not be affected by participation in the program. He would agree not to graze or to harvest any other crop from the 20 acres.

Suppose this particular 20 acres would normally have produced four hundred bushels of wheat. In return for withholding it temporarily from production, the farmer who voluntarily participates would receive a certificate, the value of which will be set at an incentive level sufficiently high to assure success of the program.

He will, in effect, have net income insurance on the 20 acres he does not plant. He will be assured income from these reserve acres even in a year of complete crop failure.

With production reduced by the amount that otherwise would have been harvested from the acres withheld—on this farm and all others—the Commodity Credit Corporation can then use part of its accumulated stocks to supply market needs. And it can do this without depressing prices for wheat farmers will be selling.

Let me express this another way: The quantities that are not produced, because farmers withhold a part of their allotted acres, will create the opportunity for a market into which the Commodity Credit Corporation can begin to disgorge its accumulations. If it unloads as much as this market will take, market prices will not be adversely affected. If it unloads somewhat less, market prices for what farmers currently produce might be expected to improve.

We would use the surplus to use up the surplus.

The voluntary reduction in plantings would be continued for perhaps three or four years. In the case of wheat we look for a cut below allotments of about 12 million acres—and in the case of cotton about 3 million acres.

This is indeed a bold plan that strikes directly at the problem. It will permit the sound agricultural program started under the Agricultural Act of 1954 to begin to function as it should.

It will remove the crushing burden of surpluses that is our most serious farm problem.

It will prevent a further diversion of acres out of surplus crops and onto other producers.

It will ease apprehension among our friends abroad over our surplus disposal program.

It will protect farm income and promote economic security.

It will reduce by many millions of dollars the storage costs on government stockpiles. If through this program we could work off 200 million bushels of wheat and 2 million bales of cotton each year for the next three years, the savings in carrying costs alone on Commodity Credit Corporation inventory would be about $400 million.

This is not a device to empty government warehouses so they may be filled again. In future years we must avoid, as we would a plague, farm programs that would encourage a build-up of new price-depressing surpluses.

The second part of the soil bank proposal is pointed both toward achieving needed adjustments in land use and over-coming some of the problems created by acres already diverted out of surplus crops. This part is called a conservation reserve.

Under the pressure of wartime incentives, large acreages have come into cultivation which sound conservation would have reserved in forage, trees, and water. We do not need these acres today in harvested crops. The wiser use of the land, particularly where it may blow or erode, is to return it to soil-conserving cover.

The conservation reserve is proposed both for these lands and for alleviating the diverted acres problem.

This also is recommended as a voluntary program. Farmers will be asked to contract with the government to shift land out of cultivated crops and into forage or trees and where feasible to ponds and reservoirs. Any farmer will be eligible to partici-pate, regardless of the crop he grows or where his farm is lo-cated. He will be paid a fair share of the cost of establishing the forage or tree cover—up to a specified maximum amount per acre that will vary for different regions. Further, as the farmer reorganizes his farm along these soil conserving lines, we recommend that the government provide certain annual pay-ments for a period of years related to the length of time needed to establish the new use of the land. Here, as in the acreage reserve program, we would not let the farmer's cooperation im-pair his historic acreage allotments.

In return the farmer will agree that any acres he puts into the conservation reserve (part two of the soil bank) will repre-sent a net reduction in his cultivated acres, and will be in addi-tion to any land he may have in the acreage reserve (part one of the soil bank). He will agree to refrain from reverting these acres to cultivated crop production—and will further agree not to graze them for a specified period of years. The grazing restriction is specifically for the protection of livestock producers, particularly cattlemen and dairymen, at this time when their production is large and their prices are depressed.

The President has expressed the hope that about 25 million acres may come into the conservation reserve program—with as much of this as possible being brought in this year.

Just as the first part of the President's soil bank proposal will bring large rewards, so likewise will this second part.

It will result in improved soil and water conservation for the benefit of both this and future generations not yet born.

It could increase our supply of timber resources on the farms and the other benefits of expanded tree cover.

It will provide immediate protection for crop producers who have been burdened by diverted acres thrust upon them.

It will alleviate the stimulus to over-rapid increases in livestock resulting from feed grain production on diverted acres.

In combination with part one of the soil bank it will help, during the next several years, to achieve a temporary reduction in total agricultural production.

I wish particularly to emphasize the temporary nature of any such reduction. In the not-so-distant future we will need much greater output of farm products than we have today. But until the surplus accumulations can be worked down, until a better balance can be reestablished between different products, some moderate drop in total output will help materially to improve prices and increase agricultural prosperity. Meantime we are storing fertility in the soil.

We can give no hard and fast estimate of how much the soil bank will improve prices and incomes. But, I repeat, our economists estimate that prices would now be perhaps 10 per cent higher than they are—if we did not have the surpluses. And they calculate that last year's farm income could have been about 20 per cent higher—a gain of more than $2 billion.

I have covered only the first point of our nine-point recommendations to the Congress. I have chosen specifically to emphasize the soil bank proposal because of its importance. We need it—and we need it now—so that we may get out from under the burden of surpluses and let our sound, long-time program started with the Agricultural Act of 1954 work as farmers and ranchers have a right to expect it to work.

The second of the President's recommendations to the Congress covered several proposals to speed up and increase our surplus-disposal activities. I intend to seek expert help from the nation's top flight executives in the merchandising fields. With their cooperation, it is my hope that we will be able to devise vigorous campaigns to move surpluses into consumption at an accelerated rate.

The third recommendation contains proposals designed to strengthen our individual commodity programs, such as corn, wheat, cotton, rice, and dairy.

The fourth item suggests that Congress may consider setting a dollar limit on the size of price-support loans to any one individual. The purpose of this suggestion is to strengthen the competitive position of our traditional family-size farms.

The fifth recommendation is prompt enactment of the rural development program designed specifically to promote the interests of our many low-income farm families.

The sixth deals with the Great Plains program directed toward the problems of improved land use and more economic farm and ranch organization in this uncertain-climate area.

Number seven calls for sharply expanded research to find new crops, new markets, new uses, to improve the efficiency of our agricultural marketing system, and to expand our backlog of fundamental scientific knowledge.

The eighth point deals with credit. We are determined that an adequate supply of credit will be available to our farmers and ranchers at all times. It is needed especially for young men, veterans particularly, who are just getting started in farming.

The final recommendation is for legislation to refund the Federal gas tax to farmers and ranchers on the gasoline they use on the farm.

Taken in its entirety the President's agricultural message embodies the changes necessary to meet honestly and straight-forwardly the farm and ranch problems of these trying times. It is a program that protects the interests and the income of the many farmers who are asked temporarily to cut production. It protects other farmers from acres that might otherwise be dumped upon them. It protects livestock producers from serious and undue competition they otherwise would have. It points toward conserving and enhancing our agricultural resources for the benefit of all—including this generation and others yet un-born. It is a program for the welfare of the family farm.

We have been earnestly studying the farm problem for many months. This nine-point program building on our present program has been developed from a broad base. It merits and will receive bipartisan support. It is designed to meet the urgent needs of our farmers today in a way consistent with our basic traditions. It offers no nostrums or panaceas. Our farm folk want none. Farmers expect programs that are economically sound and fair to all our people. They want these programs on a voluntary basis with the government cooperating not dic-tating—programs which help them to help themselves. This program meets all these requirements.

In the words of the President:

This program offers a workable approach to reducing the surpluses, bringing production and markets into balance at fair prices, and so rais-ing the income and advancing the security of our farm families.

Should this program be enacted, its degree of success will be dependent upon the degree of farmer participation and upon a common determination to work together in ridding ourselves of burdensome surpluses. With such a spirit, this program will speed the transition to a stable, prosperous, and free peacetime agriculture with a bright future.

Again I urge upon the Congress the need for swift legislative action on these recommendations, in the interest of our farm people, in the interest of every American citizen.

We appreciate your advice—your cooperation. This program is your program. With God's help we will move ahead to a brighter day for American farmers.

I pledge to you that I shall never knowingly advocate any program or policy which I believe is not in the best interest of farmers and fair to all our people—regardless of any political pressure. And I shall perform the duties that are my responsibility in full faith to the American people, as God gives me the wisdom and the strength to do.

PARTY POLITICS

I AM A CANDIDATE [1]

DWIGHT D. EISENHOWER [2]

President Dwight D. Eisenhower told the nation on Wednesday night, February 29, 1956, at ten o'clock (Eastern Standard Time), that he would be a candidate for the presidential nomination at the Republican National Convention, at San Francisco, California, on August 20. The message, delivered from the White House, with his immediate family present, was broadcast to a radio and television audience of some one hundred million.

At a White House news conference that morning the President had already revealed his decision. "My answer is positive—that is, affirmative." The twenty-minute evening talk was a detailed explanation of his reasons for this decision.

During the five months after the President was stricken with coronary thrombosis on September 24, 1955, the nation-wide and uninterrupted question was, "Will Ike run again?" Medical reports from the beginning were favorable. The latest report, that of February 15, 1956, stated that the president appeared physically fit to serve "another five to ten years" in a job like the presidency.

During this five-month time of uncertainty Republicans constantly expressed their hope and confidence that he would recover and again lead the party. The Gallup Poll, in its "anniversary audit," at the end of February 1956, showed that the President was more popular than at any time since his taking office. His popularity rating in February 1953, was 68 per cent, whereas in February 1956, the score stood at 76 per cent.

The evening address was historically unique in its subject and its personal approach. The President, aged sixty-five, talked frankly about his heart ailment. "As a recovered heart patient," he might be "a greater risk than is the normal person of my age." But, he declared, "there is not the slightest doubt that I can now perform as well as I ever have, all the important duties of the presidency."

His physical capacity to carry out these duties would inevitably become a major issue in the campaign. This problem would be coupled with the capacity of the vice-presidential candidate, presumably Richard M. Nixon, to replace the president if necessary. All domestic parties and

---

[1] The text is from the Des Moines *Register*, March 2, 1956. This transcription is identical with the copy furnished by the White House.

[2] For biographical note, see Appendix.

interests and most foreign governments expressed much satisfaction in the President's recovery and decision to continue his active Republican leadership. Republicans were jubilant. Said Governor Christian Herter, of Massachusetts, "Delighted." Former President Hoover reported, "I am certainly glad." Senator William G. Knowland, of California, who had entered the Republican primary and withdrew after the announcement, stated, "Mr. Eisenhower will be renominated by acclamation."

Adlai E. Stevenson, in the thick of his primary campaign for nomination for the presidency on the Democratic ticket, said, "It is fitting that President Eisenhower be the candidate. The main issue will be the policies and record of the Eisenhower administration. . . . Mr. Eisenhower will have to carry the burden of what will be a very vigorous campaign." He later added that President Eisenhower "spent twenty minutes Wednesday night telling the American people, not what he is going to do, but rather what he is not going to do. While I pray for his good health, I also respect a great office, which cannot be conducted on a part-time basis." [3]

My fellow citizens:

I wanted to come into your homes this evening because I feel the need of talking with you directly about a decision I made today after weeks of the most prayerful and devoutly careful consideration. I made that decision public shortly after ten this morning. Immediately I returned to this office. Upon reaching here I sat down and began to put down on paper thoughts that occurred to me which I felt might be of some interest to you in connection with that decision. This is what I wrote.

I have decided that if the Republican party chooses to renominate me I shall accept that nomination.

Thereafter, if the people of this country should elect me, I shall continue to serve them in the office I now hold. I have concluded that I should permit the American people to have the opportunity to register their decision in this matter.

In reaching this conclusion I have, first of all, been guided by the favorable reports of the doctors.

As many of you may know, their reports are that my heart has not enlarged, that my pulse and blood pressure are normal, that my blood analysis is excellent, my weight satisfactory, and I have shown no signs of undue fatigue after periods of normal mental and physical activity.

[3] See the Cumulative Author Index for references to comments on earlier speeches by President Eisenhower.

In addition, I have consulted literally with multitudes of friends and associates, either personally or through correspondence. With their advice—once I had been assured of a favorable opinion—I have diligently sought the path of personal responsibility, and of duty to the immense body of citizens who have supported me and this Administration in what we have been jointly trying to do for America.

In the last analysis, however, the decision was my own. Even the closest members of my family have declined to urge me to any specific course, merely saying that they would cheerfully abide by whatever I decided was best to do.

From the moment that any man is first elected President of the United States, there is continuous public interest in the question as to whether or not he will seek reelection.

In most instances, presidents in good health have sought, or at least have made themselves available for, a second term.

In my own case this question, which was undecided before my recent illness, has been complicated by the heart attack I suffered on September 24 last year.

Aside from all other considerations, I have been faced with the fact that I am classed as a recovered heart patient. This means that to some undetermined extent, I may possibly be a greater risk than is the normal person of my age. My doctors assure me that this increased percentage of risk is not great.

So far as my own personal sense of well-being is concerned, I am as well as before the attack occurred.

It is, however, true that the opinions and conclusions of the doctors that I can continue to carry the burdens of the presidency, contemplate for me a regime of ordered work activity, interspersed with regular amounts of exercise, recreation and rest.

A further word about this prescribed regime. I must keep my weight at a proper level. I must take a short mid-day breather. I must normally retire at a reasonable hour, and I must eliminate many of the less important social and ceremonial activities.

But let me make one thing clear. As of this moment, there is not the slightest doubt that I can now perform as well as I ever have, all of the important duties of the presidency. This I say because I am actually doing so and have been doing so for many weeks.

Of course, the duties of the President are essentially endless. No daily schedule of appointments can give a full timetable—or even a faint indication—of the President's responsibilities.

Entirely aside from the making of important decisions, there is the formulation of policy through the national security council and the Cabinet, cooperation with the Congress and with the states; there is for the President a continuous burden of study, contemplation and reflection.

Of the subjects demanding this endless study, some deal with foreign affairs, with the position of the United States in the international world, her strength, her aspirations, and the methods by which she may exert her influence in the solution of world problems and in the direction of a just and enduring peace. These—all of them—are a particular constitutional responsibility of the President.

These subjects, requiring study and contemplation, include, also, major questions affecting our economy, the relationships of our government to our people, the Federal Government's role in assuring our citizens medical and educational facilities, and important economic and social policies in a variety of fields.

The president is the constitutional commander in chief of our armed forces and is constantly confronted with major questions as to their efficiency, organization, operations, and adequacy.

All these matters, among others, are with a President always; in Washington, in a summer White House, on a weekend absence, indeed, even at a ceremonial dinner and in every hour of leisure. The old saying is true, "A President never escapes from his office."

These are the things to which I refer when I say I am now carrying the duties of the President. So far as I am concerned, I am confident that I can continue to carry them indefinitely.

Otherwise, I would never have made the decision I announced today.

The doctors insist that hard work of the kind I have described does not injure any recovered coronary case, if such a recovered patient will follow the regime they lay down. Certainly, to this moment, the work has not hurt me.

Readiness to obey the doctors, out of respect for my present duties and responsibilities, is mandatory in my case. I am now doing so, and I intend to continue doing so for the remainder of my life, no matter in what capacity I may be living or may be serving.

Incidentally, some of my medical advisers believe that adverse effects on my health will be less in the presidency than in any other position I might hold.

They believe that because of the watchful care that doctors can and do exercise over a President, he normally runs less risk of physical difficulty than do other citizens.

The fact is probably of more importance to my family than to the nation at large, but believing you may have some interest in the point, I wanted to inform you.

Now, with this background of fact, and medical opinion and belief, what do these circumstances imply in terms of restrictions upon the activities in which I have been accustomed to participate in the past?

During the first two and a half years of my incumbency, I felt that a great effort was needed in America to clarify our own thinking with respect to problems of international peace and our nation's security; the proper relationships of the Federal Government with the states; the relationship of the Federal Government to our economy and to individual citizens; increased cooperation of the executive branch with the Congress; problems of the nation's farmers; the need for highways; the building of schools; the extension of social welfare; and a myriad of other items of similar importance.

To this public clarification of issues I devoted much time and effort. In many cases these things can now be done equally well by my close associates, but in others I shall continue to perform these important tasks.

Some of the things in which I can properly have a reduced schedule include public speeches, office appointments with individuals and with groups, ceremonial dinners, receptions, and other portions of a very heavy correspondence.

Likewise I have done a great deal of traveling, much of which was undertaken in the effort to keep in personal touch with the thinking of you, the people of America. Both in war and in peace, it has been my conviction that no man can isolate himself from the men and women he is attempting to serve, and really sense what is in their hearts and minds.

This kind of activity I shall continue, but not on such an intensive basis that I must violate the restrictions within which I must work.

All this means, also, that neither for renomination nor reelection would I engage in extensive traveling and in whistle-stop speaking—normally referred to as "barnstorming."

I had long ago made up my mind, before I ever dreamed of a personal heart attack, that I could never, as President of all the people, conduct that kind of political campaign where I was personally a candidate. The first duty of a President is to discharge to the limit of his ability, the responsibilities of his office.

On the record are the aims, the efforts, the accomplishments and the plans for the future of this Administration. Those facts constitute my personal platform.

I put all these things clearly before you for two reasons.

The first is that every delegate attending the Republican convention next August is entitled to know now that, for all the reasons I have given, I shall, in general, wage no political campaign in the customary pattern.

Instead, my principal purpose, if renominated, will be to inform the American people accurately, through means of mass communication, of the foreign and domestic program this Administration has designed and has pressed for the benefit of all our people.

If the Republican delegates come to believe that they should have as their presidential nominee one who would campaign more actively, they would have the perfect right—indeed the duty—to name such a nominee.

I, for one, would accept their decision cheerfully and I would continue by all means within my power to help advance the interests of the American people through the kind of program that this Administration has persistently supported.

The second reason for placing these things before you is because I am determined that every American shall have all available facts concerning my personal condition and the way I am now conducting the affairs of this office. Thus, when they go to the polls next November to elect a President of the United States, they can, should I again be one of the nominees, do so with a full understanding of both the record of this Administration and of how I propose to conduct myself now and in the future.

I know of little that I can add to this statement. As I hope all of you know, I am dedicated to a program that rigidly respects the concepts of political and economic freedom on which this nation was founded, that holds there must be equal justice and equality of opportunity for individuals, that adapts governmental methods to changing industrial, economic and social conditions, and that has, as its never changing purpose, the welfare, prosperity, and above all, the security of 166 million Americans.

The work that I set out four years ago to do has not yet reached the state of development and fruition that I then hoped could be accomplished within the period of a single term in this office.

So if the American people choose, under the circumstances I have described, to place this duty upon me, I shall persist in the way that has been charted by my associates and myself.

I shall continue, with earnestness, sincerity and enthusiasm, to discharge the duties of this office.

Now my friends, I have earnestly attempted to give the most important facts and considerations which I took into account in reaching the decision I announced today. If I have omitted anything significant, it is something I shall strive to correct in the weeks ahead.

Thank you very much for permitting me to visit with you this evening on this very important matter. Good night to all of you.

THE REPUBLICAN CAUSE IN 1956 [4]

RICHARD M. NIXON [5]

Vice President Richard M. Nixon, just arrived from his speech-making at the inauguration of President Juscelino Kubitschek, of Brazil, gave this address at the seventieth annual Lincoln Day dinner, of the National Republican Club, at the Waldorf-Astoria, New York City, on Monday evening, February 13, 1956.

The address was nationally broadcast via radio-television, by the Columbia Broadcasting System.

Ex-Governor Thomas E. Dewey introduced the speaker. Mr. Nixon, in recognition of his services to the Administration and the nation, was presented with a bronze head of Lincoln.

The speech was strongly pro-Republican and set the framework of issues for the coming campaign. The accomplishments of Eisenhower's three years were summarized, and the current Democratic criticisms were refuted. Had the Republican policy led to the "brink" of war? Said Mr. Nixon, better at the brink than in the drink. Was the GOP the party of the "big fellow" to the neglect of the little one? Mr. Nixon's reply: The 65 million wage earners were never so well off. What of the weakness of the GOP in social security and civil rights? Republicans, said Nixon, had led in the extending of civil rights. Republican Supreme Court Justice Earl Warren had been spokesman for the decree outlawing school segregation.

Absent in the speech was any grappling with one major issue—agricultural relief.

Notable were the speaker's personal proofs—his tribute to the cabinet and especially to President Eisenhower, likened to Lincoln.

Mr. Nixon's arguments and appeals were similar to those he developed so vigorously in the campaign of 1954. Again the motives were (1) peace and security, (2) economic well being, (3) social and personal satisfactions, (4) assured defense against outside foes (communism), and (5) confidence in that great leader Eisenhower. The vividness of the language and clear organization of the discourse contributed to this persuasiveness. The delivery, too, was energetic. The voice and words sometimes approached the emotional elevation of oratory. Mr. Nixon's voice and articulation before the microphone could well match those of

---

[4] Permission for this reprint granted through the courtesy of Vice President Richard M. Nixon. The text is from the New York *Times*, February 14, 1956. p 18.

[5] For biographical note, see Appendix.

that other excellent campaigner, Thomas Dewey. The audience applause was frequent and enthusiastic.

The next day Southern Democratic senators, including John Stennis, of Mississippi, and Samuel Ervin, of North Carolina, denounced Mr. Nixon for putting Chief Justice Warren and the Supreme Court desegregation issue "right in the middle of the forthcoming political campaign." Democratic Senator Hubert Humphrey, of Minnesota, said, "I didn't know that the Supreme Court was Republican or Democratic."[6]

Governor Dewey, President [Daniel J.] Riesner, all of the distinguished guests in back of me and all of the distinguished guests here in this audience: May I tell you first some of the reasons why appearing before this National Republican Club's Lincoln Day dinner is such a special privilege for me.

And the first is one that you have just witnessed. Because New York has given the Republican party not only one of the greatest governors in our nation's history, but also a man who with such high courage and dedication and dignity was the Republican standard bearer in two national campaigns, the man who was awarded this very award I received last year—Governor Dewey.

And second because New York has given to the Republican National Committee in Len Hall a man who as national chairman has done a job I say unsurpassed in history by any chairman of either major political party.

And third, this is for the consumption only of our people in here in the New York audience, because I believe that in order to compensate for a quite expensive political accident temporarily occupying the Governor's Mansion in Albany, I know that New York Republicans will this November give a Republican colleague to a great Republican Senator, Irving Ives; that you will increase your splendid twenty-six-man Republican delegation in the House, and that you will assure, and this is important, an even greater majority for the Republican candidate for President than you did in 1952, and you did a great job then.

Now as reference has been made several times this evening, this is the seventieth annual Lincoln's Birthday Dinner sponsored by this great Republican organization. And [in] those years—

[6] For further comment on Richard M. Nixon as speaker, see *Representative American Speeches: 1954-55*, p89-98.

and some in this audience can remember many of them—our party has seen so many great days. But I say never since the days of Lincoln himself has the Republican party had a greater moment, nor a better cause to present to the people, than it has today.

And I say that for these reasons: first because of what we've done; and second because of what we stand for; and third because of our leadership.

Let's examine first the magnificent record of the first three years of what all of us hope will be the eight years of the Eisenhower Administration.

You remember what we found three years ago.

There was war in Korea.

Federal controls stifled our nation's economy.

Every day the people's take-home pay, pensions and insurance were buying less and less at the corner store.

And all over Washington plans were under way to socialize and federalize America's farmers, the medical profession, housing, schools and power, including the new-found power of the atom.

Most distressing of all, a great majority of the American people, Democrats and Republicans alike, had lost faith in the honesty, the integrity and the reliability of those who served them in government. That was three years ago.

Now after just three years of Eisenhower leadership and policy we find this situation.

For the first time in fifteen years the whole world is at peace.

Our economy has been freed from the dead hand of Federal control.

The American people have had the biggest tax cut in history.

For the first time since the Republican Eightieth Congress we not only have already achieved a balanced budget this year, but our Republican President has submitted a balanced budget for next year as well.

And what is the result? What is the result? And that is the importance as far as these policies are concerned. The result is that through these Republican economic policies America today is enjoying its greatest prosperity in history with gross national product, personal income, consumer expenditures, individual assets, scores of other economic indicators at . . . [an all-time] high.

And I can assure you that the plans we found for socializing America's institutions have been filed in the wastebasket, and if the Democratic Congress does even a halfway job, I can also assure you that the Eisenhower program, offered in the State of the Union message this year, will produce more schools, more highways, more hospitals, more child welfare services, more medical research, more health insurance, better working conditions, higher wage standards and more homes, than our predecessors ever dreamed of.

And, probably most important of all in those three years we have restored dignity and honesty and integrity and dependability in public service in Washington, D.C.

Now, on the basis of this record, I am going to make some rather categorical claims even for a Republican Lincoln Day dinner.

Never has an Administration kept its promises more faithfully than this Administration.

Never has an Administration done a better job for all the people than this Administration.

Never have the American people had more reason to be grateful for the leadership of a President than they have for President Eisenhower's leadership today.

And, I say further that because in so short a time it has so far advanced the best interests of all our people, regardless of party, I say the Republican party is in truth the majority party of America today.

Now there are, of course, those who do not share our enthusiasm for this record. But in the long history of American political campaigns never have we heard criticisms in my opinion that have been more negative, more contradictory, more petty, than those being offered by the leading Democratic candidates for the presidency, who in my opinion can best be described as "three candidates in search of a crisis."

For example, the Eisenhower-Dulles foreign policy seems to be their favorite target at the moment.

And since they can't agree among themselves as to what is wrong with that policy, let's examine the case being made against it by the leading Democratic candidate for the presidency, Mr. Stevenson (with apologies to Mr. De Sapio of course, I should say).

We find Mr. Stevenson has trouble even agreeing with himself. Of course, I don't believe we should be too hard on him, because I know what a difficult time he must be having to find any honest legitimate grounds on which to criticize President Eisenhower and his leadership today.

But I will suggest this: that unless he changes his present course, it will begin to look as if the state which gave the nation Abraham Lincoln, the great rail-splitter of 1860, has produced in Adlai Stevenson the great hair-splitter of 1956.

Consider these facts: He complained about the President's meeting at Geneva with what he termed a "third-string Communist leader," but now he suggests there might be some merit in negotiating a security pact with the Communists.

He says on the one hand that we're too strong, we're too weak, we're too firm and we're too flexible, we're too belligerent, we're too timid. And lately he shrinks at the suggestion that the United States may have found it necessary to be on the brink of war in order to keep the peace.

Now, this is not the time or the place to examine our foreign policy in detail, but these claims I think I can make without fear of contradiction:

The test of failure or success of foreign policy is whether it results in war or peace—and I am sure that 165 million Americans will agree with me when I say it's a lot better to be on the brink than in the drink as far as war is concerned.

And that, in the final analysis, is the big difference between the Truman-Acheson policy and the Eisenhower-Dulles policy: The Truman-Acheson policy got us into war; the Eisenhower-Dulles policy got us out.

Now, this, in essence, may I say to you, is what I conceive the Eisenhower-Dulles policy to be:

President Eisenhower was elected on a pledge to stop the war in Korea. He kept that promise and he's done more. He avoided our participation in war in Indo-China and in Formosa [Taiwan]. And at Geneva he led the whole world away from the possibility of atomic warfare. And today he is giving of his strength and his wisdom and his faith to the end that a just and abiding peace in the world may be achieved for all mankind.

Our policy is a policy of peace, peace without surrender, peace without appeasement, peace without abandonment of the enslaved peoples of Europe and Asia, peace with strength controlled by wisdom and restraint supported by the will and the power of America and the free world.

And I would suggest that if Mr. Stevenson or his colleagues have nothing more constructive to offer than criticism, that they join with millions of their fellow Democrats in this country and some of the outstanding Democrats in the Congress of the United States who have so loyally supported, and are supporting now the Eisenhower-Dulles policy—a policy which deserves support. Why? Because it got us out of one war, it kept us out of others, and it provides the best chance for peace without surrender in the years ahead.

Now there's a second major ground of criticism of the Republican Administration—I think most of you have heard it or read it—is that it is for the big fellow, we're against the little fellow; we're for the employer, we're against the worker; we're for the rich, we're against the poor.

As a great Democratic Governor of New York, Al Smith, used to say, "Let's look at the record." And let's look at the record solely in terms of the 65 million American wage earners. Has this Administration been good or bad for them?

What does he want, this wage earner? He wants a job. He wants high wages. He wants purchasing power. He wants a sound security program for the future. And he wants a government that he can trust and respect.

What does he have? Today America's wage earners have: more jobs at higher wages, with greater purchasing power, sounder security and fewer strikes than at any time in history. And they have peace and a government that they can know, that they can trust, to boot. That is what they have.

May I respectfully suggest that I don't believe we need fear the participation of union leaders in the next campaign. Because every union leader should be interested only in one thing —the welfare of the members of his union. Let each of them apply this test—under which Administration have union members had it the best?

And they will find that union members are better off today than they've ever been in the history of unions. And I submit that if they act on the basis of what has proved to be best for their members, every union leader in America will be out shouting from the housetops this November for four more years of the Eisenhower Administration.

To put it in a nutshell, I should say our Republican Administration is now proving, for the first time in nearly twenty years— thirty years—that we can have prosperity without war, full employment outside of uniform and security without regimentation and control. And we're proud of that record, and we believe that the American people, whom we represent, are proud of it too.

Now at the outset tonight I said we could be proud not only of what we've done, but also of what we stand for.

At this moment would you permit [me] to philosophize a moment about our party and what it stands for.

More and more these days we hear that there's no real difference between the two parties. But there are differences and they are very important to every citizen. To find them we, of course, must take note of the fact that we are also alike.

Both of our parties, for example, want ours to be a healthy and a happy nation daily growing stronger in every way.

But, though our parties are alike in many important ways, beneath this harmony the parties are very different in how they see each individual citizen.

We, of course, must always identify when we're speaking of the Democratic party which Democratic party we are referring to. And for the moment let us define the Democratic party in terms of its ADA [Americans for Democratic Action], big city boss clique which controls its national conventions.

That Democratic party, I submit, has lost track of the individual. It has become the slave of doctrines of uniformity, mediocrity and regimentation. In its eyes our people have dissolved into a multitude to be politically manipulated and managed, and the government, an all-wise aristocracy, rules the common people, and they will obediently plod along as they are told. The individual has been swallowed up, in other words, in a herd of unknowns.

We see this philosophy showing up all the time in Democratic pronouncements. There is endless emphasis upon the averageness of Americans. There is steady appeal to mass and to class.

And so, in a sort of helpless way, we find that this great wing of the Democratic party grinds out policies that are in fact what?—in fact reactionary. Often they amaze the still uninfected Democrats, most of whom voted for President Eisenhower in 1952, just as much as they disturb Republicans.

Now what is the difference? We Republicans reject this "managed masses" idea of these Democrats. We consider it repugnant to American tradition. It is not what true liberals believe in. Americans are not a milling mass. Our society's purpose is to fulfill the aspirations not of the middle class, not of the lower class, not of the rich or the powerful, but to fulfill the aspirations of Mary and John, of Margaret and Jim, of individual Americans whatever their status.

And to these ends we must keep each individual as free as possible. How do we do this? We must keep a tight halter on the powers of government. Because such a government in turn must largely depend on individual and local resolution of public problems. And that is why we Republicans fight every unnecessary encroachment upon individual liberty.

And so there we have the great fundamental of our party: We hold high the liberal standard of individual freedom.

And we clearly see the opposite as well—the Democratic addiction to reactionary mass and class ideas in which individualism tends to wither and die.

Now there's another big difference between our party and the big city machine, left-wing alliance which for twenty-four years has named and controlled Democratic candidates for the

presidency—and will do so again this year. It's in the ability of
the parties to reach the goals we all believe in. Attorney General Javits has already referred to this.

Because perhaps in no other field is there a greater contrast
between Democratic campaign promises and Democratic congressional performance than with respect to civil rights and race
relations.

Why just the other day out in my home state of California,
Mr. Stevenson and Mr. Kefauver talked about it again and, as
usual, they contradicted each other and then each of them contradicted himself.

And despite the unquestioned good intentions of some of
those in the Northern wing of their party the Democrats know
that their hybrid party is helpless and futile in this field and
that it will stay that way.

And they know something else. They know that President
Eisenhower's Republican Administration has registered the
greatest advance for the rights of racial minorities since the
Emancipation Proclamation itself.

We've abolished racial segregation in the District of Columbia, in the armed forces and in Federal contracts and civilian
employment.

Through the Interstate Commerce Commission we've abolished
racial discrimination in travel by bus, and boat, and rail.

And, speaking for a unanimous Supreme Court, a great Republican Chief Justice, Earl Warren, has ordered an end to racial
segregation in the nation's schools.

And we did this, mind you, we did this all in just three
years. And I say that the only hope for continued progress
toward the realization of the American dream, the dream that
we always think of on Lincoln's Birthday particularly, the dream
of equal opportunity in every respect for every American, is
through the election not only of a Republican President but a
Republican House and Senate this November, and we give you
that job.

And might I add one further word as to what we consider
our party stands for. I believe we can all be thankful tonight
that President Eisenhower has given the Republican party the

forward look. It's our New Deal friends who are now trapped by their own reactionary philosophy, they're wailing at the wall for a return to discredited economic policies which never provided and never will provide prosperity except in time of war.

Now I realize that there are some even in our party who might criticize this Administration on the ground that it's too liberal, too progressive. But let us consider the alternative. The choice is not between the Eisenhower program and something more conservative but between the Eisenhower program and something far more radical.

And let us also consider this fact. The American people are not going to stand still. They want progress. They want an Administration which doesn't look to the past, they want one that isn't satisfied with the present, but they want one which by deeds even more than words shows the way to new and greater hope for the future.

Now some may ask how then do we differ from our Democratic friends in this respect? It's a very simple but a very important difference.

We believe that the road to progress is through programs which rely primarily upon individual rather than government enterprise. We believe that government can and should be progressive and humanitarian without being socialistic. And that's a difference we're very proud of; it's one that we are carrying out in this Administration.

It seems to me that the birthday of the first Republican President is a particularly appropriate time for us all to remind ourselves of a fact that if we studied history carefully we would not need to be reminded of. And that is that the Republican party in its greatest days has always been, and it is now, and it will continue to be the party of progress for America.

Finally, I think we can be proud as Republicans tonight not only because of what we've done and what we stand for but because of the leadership we offer to the nation and to the world.

May I say a word first about the Cabinet to which New York has made such a significant contribution in our splendid Secretary of State and Attorney General.

When our opponents charge that this is a businessman's Administration, I don't believe we should back away or apologize. This is an answer: The Government of the United States is the biggest business in the world. And as such, President Eisenhower believes it ought to have the best management in the world.

And I say that no achievement of this Administration has been more in the national interest than getting seasoned and tested practical leaders of the caliber of Secretaries Humphrey and Wilson and Weeks, and scores like them, to come to Washington to provide the kind of management that gives to Americans the most return in services from every tax dollar they invest. To that extent we are a business Administration.

I have spoken of the Cabinet, of the President's official family. There is very little that I can add about President Eisenhower's personal leadership which has not already been better said by the eloquent speakers who have preceded me on the platform and which has not already been said perhaps far more eloquently on January 20 at the "Salute to Eisenhower" dinners in which New York—and congratulations to all of you who participated at it—played such a splendid part.

But may I say what I believe is in the hearts of the great majority of Americans tonight regardless of party as far as their President is concerned. There are a number of reasons we love and admire our President.

Certainly because he has given the inspired leadership which has brought America the greatest peace and prosperity and progress that any people have ever enjoyed in this history of nations.

But most of all because of the man he is. Americans like to be proud of the man in the White House. And in our history we've been fortunate in having some great presidents. Some have been Republicans. Some have been Democrats. And our first Republican President, Abraham Lincoln, was one of the greatest. And today we have a man cast in that same great mold in President Eisenhower.

And we know that we need never fear that he will debase his high office by deeds or words which are cheap or crude or petty. We know he will not deliberately misrepresent or distort for political goals. We know that we can always proudly hold this President of the United States up to our children as a man who has faith in God, faith in America, and one who has brought dignity and respect and integrity to the highest office in the land.

And for such a glowing record, for such a truly liberal philosophy, for such a great man, we can be thankful tonight. And there's a way we can show our appreciation and that way is by our dedication to winning the victory this November which will assure continuation of the policies and leadership which to the great majority of our people have brought the best three years of our lives.

SCORING THE REPUBLICAN RECORD [7]

ADLAI E. STEVENSON [8]

Adlai E. Stevenson gave this campaign speech on November 19, 1955, at the Stock Yards Convention Hall (Amphitheatre Hall), Chicago, Illinois. The occasion was a fund-raising dinner ($100 per plate), the climax of a four-day session of the Democratic National Committee. Some 2800 attended the dinner and more than $240,000 was netted.

Mr. Stevenson, who on November 15 had announced his candidacy for the nomination for the presidency, was the main speaker. His address was broadcast and televised nationally. Other speakers included Senator Estes Kefauver of Tennesse, Governor Averell Harriman of New York, and former President Harry S. Truman.

This Chicago speech, the harbinger of Stevenson's aggressive campaign utterances in the state primaries of California, Minnesota, and elsewhere, and in the later campaign itself, outlined again the basic issues on which the campaign would be waged. Under sharp indictment were the Republican three-year record on foreign affairs, the Washington domestic policies in the interest of "big" business and industry, vacillating farm administration, sabotaging of public power contracts, failures in general public services (e.g., education), and opposition to free collective bargaining.

Stevenson, often criticized because his 1952 campaign appeals had not hit the Republicans deeply enough, gave at Chicago a hard-driving attack that evoked much audience enthusiasm. But Stevenson's platform manner and language continued to be those of a statesman rather than those of a blunt rear-platform campaigner.

Criticism from both Republicans and Democratic radicals quickly followed. Harold Stassen, Eisenhower's disarmament aide, upon his return from Europe on November 20, said that the Stevenson speeches, including this latest one, were beginning to affect adversely the American overseas policies. The Europeans "are puzzled and perplexed by Mr. Stevenson's recent voice of strange dissent in our policy." (Stevenson's Chicago criticism of our foreign policy was not as specific nor as denunciatory as was Kefauver's on that program.) Democratic left-wingers also denounced the Stevenson speech as too compromising—for example, his plea for a policy of "moderation."

[7] Text as reported in the New York *Times,* November 20, 1955, p66. The text was also supplied to this editor by the Democratic National Committee and reprinted here through the courtesy of Mr. Adlai Stevenson.

[8] For biographical note, see Appendix.

Gallup and other polls, nevertheless, continued to rate Stevenson far in the lead over other possible Democratic nominees. His excellent television personality, political wisdom, originality of phrasing, and general communicative effectiveness sustained the reputation for high platform ability he had acquired in the 1952 and 1954 campaigns.[9]

Mayor Daley, President Truman, my fellow Democrats, whom I am honored to welcome to Illinois, to Chicago and to the International Amphitheatre once again.

I thought I had a good speech for you here tonight but I've discovered that it has a serious defect—among the nine preceding speakers you have already heard it.

Our business here tonight is politics, and I propose to get right down to business.

We mean by "politics," the people's business—the most important business there is.

We mean the conduct of the people's business by all of the people, in open meetings where we can say what we think, and what we think should be done—about what we think!

For the past three days leaders of the Democratic party have met here in Chicago to discuss plans for the coming year. The discussion has been of policies and of principles—not of men. The happy truth, and it has been demonstrated here tonight by the words of President Truman, of Governor Harriman, of Senator Kefauver, of Mayor Daley, of national committeeman Jack Arvey, of Chairman Butler, is that the Democratic party maintains an essential unity of purpose which does not depend upon the individuals who may carry its standard. And I could add that no other political party, can make that claim!

In these three days we have heard the reports of Democratic leaders from all parts of the country. The reports add up to this: That we are going to win in 1956!

We are going to win next year just as we won the special congressional elections in 1953, just as we won nine more governors and the Congress in 1954 and just as we won last week's municipal elections.

[9] See the Cumulative Author Index for references to comments on earlier speeches by Adlai E. Stevenson.

Indeed, as a matter of fact, Mr. President, it looks like a cinch if we could only get out the vote of those new Democratic mayors.

This is what I wanted to talk about here tonight—what we Democrats are for, and, what we are against. I shall be speaking not so much to you as for you—trying to say some of the things I know are in all of our hearts and minds, the things that give us the right to call ourselves Democrats—and Americans.

We propose not to make issues where there are none, nor to be critical without being constructive. Our disagreement with the central principles of Republican policy runs deep, but it does not diminish our respect for those who sincerely hold that political faith. We respect the leader of the Republican party, President Eisenhower, who is President for Democrats as well as for Republicans, and we rejoice alike in the progress of his recovery.

Our first, our greatest, our most relentless purpose is peace. For without peace, there is nothing.

And now that the mists of illusion have risen from last summer's meeting at the "summit" we must again face the fact that the cold war is still in the deep freeze; that our security system is deteriorating, and that a safe and orderly world is still a distant goal. Certainly we must have learned by now that peace and security cannot be had for the asking, or by slogans and tough talk, or by blowing alternately hot and cold, rash and prudent. Certainly we must have learned that sound foreign policies cannot be devised with one eye fixed only on the budget, and the other on the divisions in the Republican party. Certainly we must have learned that in the fluctuating market of world affairs there is no bargain basement where peace can be had cheap.

But let us be very clear that Republicans want a safe and a sane world every bit as much as Democrats. And in this day, when our position is more perilous than it has been since Korea, let us also profit from our past mistakes, and let us think of foreign policy not as partisans but as Americans. Let us, indeed, remember that who plays with politics, who plays politics with peace will lose at both.

Our world is dominated by two formidable facts—expansive Communist imperialism with the hydrogen bomb in its arsenal,

and the great revolutionary upsurge of the less privileged peoples
who long for peace and for a share in the better things of life.

These simple facts present a complex challenge. We and our
allies must be strong to check Communist expansion. Yet we
cannot allow fear or envy or frustration to alienate the vast mass
of the uncommitted peoples.

Unhappily, this balance, so painstakingly created under President Truman, has not been preserved. America's military strength
has been reduced—while at the same time we talked louder and
tougher. But if our threats were sincere then our pretensions of
peace were insincere. And if we did not mean what we said,
then we were bluffing.

Small wonder that distrust and fear of us became so widespread that the world received with profound relief President
Eisenhower's assurances at Geneva last summer that America was
really and truly a peaceful nation.

We must restore the balance in America's relations with the
world—the balance between our strength and our concern. To
guard the ramparts of freedom we must uphold the stability of
our alliances. We must maintain our military strength. But mar-
tial strength is not an end in itself. It can be only the firm base
from which we are prepared to negotiate, whenever negotiation
seems fruitful, and from which we will seek to create with tire-
less patience a workable system of controlled disarmament.

To this restored vision of a firm, a consistent, a peace-loving
America, we must add a refreshed concern for our less fortunate
neighbors. We must play our generous part in the bettering of
the human lot; and we must do so not just to compete with
communism, not to preserve colonialism, not to impose Ameri-
canism. We must make the world understand again what it once
knew so well—that at the roots of our American faith we recognize that we belong, all of us, to the family of man.

And here at home, no less than in our foreign affairs, primary
importance attaches to the genuineness of our concern for human
welfare. It is the fundamental faith of our party that in a democracy the individual citizen is all-important—that ordinary men
and women have the sense, the integrity and the decency to make
choices and to decide for themselves how best to improve their

lot and how best to use their human span. Our aim is simply to secure the widest distribution of well-being. And we know that this can only happen when responsibility for policy making and participation in government is also widely shared.

The sense of democracy as a partnership in which all of our people share and participate has been blurred in these past three years. Instead, in whatever direction we look—tax policy, regulatory policy, resources policy, credit policy, or what not—we see the sharp outlines of what can only be described as special-interest government in Washington, something we haven't seen since the Republicans were there last! We are coming, I think, to realize that we are being treated more as customers than as partners—gullible customers, susceptible to the huckstering advertiser arts of salesmen for a special interest.

Well, you know that the people own this business, and they don't want anybody to forget it. We Americans climbed, together, from the trough of depression which we Democrats had inherited from the Republicans. And today most Americans dwell upon the plateau of prosperity which the Republicans inherited from us.

And even though they had never had it so good, the Republicans promised a lot of changes back in 1952. Personally, Mr. President, I don't know why we Democrats complain so much about their broken campaign promises. It's the promises that they keep that hurt us. Every change that they've made has caused us trouble, but the things they haven't changed are working just fine.

Among other things they adopted a new farm policy—to get rid, they say, of the farm surpluses. Well, it hasn't reduced the farmer's production, but it has sure reduced his income. And today the only reason we have a stable general price level to which the Republicans point with such pride is that rising industrial prices are offset by falling farm prices. The balance, the all-important balance in our interdependent economy is threatened, and the well-being of twenty million Americans is sinking, while the Republican cheer leaders shout: "Everything is booming but the guns."

Our society needs the farmer more than anyone else. And the farmer needs a fair share of the national income. He hasn't got it just now. And there is precious little evidence that the "team" in Washington wants to do anything much about it. But to help the farmer in this passing crisis you have to want to help the farmer.

But I hear, my friends, there may be a change. I hear that farm prices are not the only thing that's flexible about Republican politicians, and it is no secret that they are now dusting off some of the old Democratic production control proposals with a view to bringing them out—under Republican labels, of course. It is strange what an election year does to those crusaders who believe so devoutly in good old-fashioned, rugged individualism —especially for the farmer.

In our natural resources policy there has also been a change— an attempt to undermine our conservation and power programs which are serving the interests of millions of people—particularly small consumers.

Today's fast dollar is being put above tomorrow's needs— Hell's Canyon goes to a private company for only partial development; an effort is made to sabotage the preference clause in our public power contracts, and to cripple the great rural electrification program; the dubious Dixon-Yates deal is contrived in secrecy and the TVA is attacked publicly.

This Republican inability to make a proper distinction between public and private business shows up elsewhere. We hear now about waste and privilege in the housekeeping department of the government. We hear that the Secretary of the Air Force is decorated for his services after getting his public and his private affairs embarrassingly mixed up—while at the same time thousands of honest and conscientious Government workers, littler people, have been coldly pushed around so that the crusaders could boast about cleaning something up.

And surely one of the most remarkable alibis in years was offered last week by another high level administrator who found it convenient to resign; admittedly he pressed his company's claims against the Government—but only, he insists, on his lunch hour!

I have been wondering what goes on down there during the coffee break.

As Democrats we deny the soundness of helping only the large corporations with the pious hope that something will trickle down for the rest of us. We oppose special tax advantages to anyone, let alone to a favored few. We oppose the policy of giving the lion's share of defense contracts to the large companies.

And twenty years of Democratic leadership went into making America economically strong by increasing and broadening and stabilizing consumer buying power. And we still claim that the best thing for any business is people coming in the door with money in their pockets.

I suggest that this whole pattern is a reflection of the basic philosophy our new managers brought to Washington in 1953. "We are here," you will recall, the Secretary of the Interior said, "as an Administration representing business and industry." Well, after three years I'm convinced that that gentleman knew what he was talking about!

Let us be quite clear about this. There is no conflict between the Democrats and business. What we criticize is not business, but the virtual exclusion of everyone else. Eight of the ten members of the Cabinet and almost three quarters of the men appointed to high executive policy-forming office in the past three years come from the same segment of the community, big business. Is this a good thing? I doubt it, and I suspect businessmen by and large doubt it, too.

We do not question the honesty of these men, we don't question their good intentions, we don't question their right to hold office. But we do question the breadth and the variety of their collective vision; we say that this republic is imperiled when government, which belongs to all the people, falls into the hands of any single group.

What do we Democrats mean to do about this when we take up the reins of government once again? I think you could sum up our aim very simply—we mean to return the public interest to the center of public policy. We mean to restore the sense that government is the concern not of a single dominant economic interest but of all the American people.

But there are those among us who say, let well enough alone, all is well, don't rock the boat. And I agree that this is an age of abundance, as well as an age of anxiety. I agree that it is time for catching our breath; I agree that moderation is the spirit of the times. But we must take care lest we confuse moderation with mediocrity, lest we settle for half answers to hard problems. A democratic society can't stand still, and the world in which we live won't stand still. Both are living things and the meaning of life is in growth, in working always toward something better, toward something higher. Moderation, yes. But stagnation, no! As the history of the rise and fall of nations before us reminds us, nothing fails like success.

We must tackle the problem of agriculture. We are committed, as I say, to restoring farm income to fair levels, by, I hope, a many-pronged attack.

Democrats don't contend that price supports, firm or collapsible, are the whole answer to a healthy farm economy. On the contrary, we have always contended, as we do now, that price supports should be employed in conjunction with other supplementary and complementary measures. The real key to the farmer's welfare is an intelligent, a sensitive, a responsive administration of agriculture on a day-to-day basis—and that is something which can only be accomplished by the party which is in office and which is genuinely concerned with the farmer's welfare.

We will seek to protect the place of small business in our free enterprise system. Enterprise depends upon opportunity— opportunity for a man with talent, with energy to branch out on his own—to build his own business, own his own plant, take his own risks, make his own decisions. And at the rate that smaller businesses are going bankrupt or being swallowed up by bigger ones you can't help but be anxious about the future of enterprise as we have understood it.

We will give urgent consideration to the plight of sub-standard families, and of the blighted or depressed areas—the stagnant pools into which the tide of prosperity has failed to flow.

We will continue to fight to preserve the nation's heritage of natural resources—our sources of power, our public lands, our national forests, our soil, our parks. We propose, very simply, to reinstate the principles which for forty years underpinned a bipartisan conservation policy initiated by Theodore Roosevelt, and interrupted for the first time in 1953.

We will attempt to bring our great public services back into balance with our expanding wealth. For, I ask you, are we really prosperous when our national income is going up but our schools are becoming more crowded, our teachers more outnumbered, our hospitals more inadequate, our roads more dangerous, our conservation more timid, our slums more contagious? Sure, the figures on the pay check are important, but is a family really prosperous if it lives in an urban jungle where juvenile delinquency takes growing children for its prey?

We Democrats are for a country in which the schools are worthy of the children—and adequately staffed by teachers supported as their honored profession merits.

We are for a country where no man's home is blighted by smoke and cut off from sunlight and air.

We are for a country where no family lives in dread of crippling disease that adds to the pain of the stricken the fear of intolerable expense.

We are for a country where older people are not doomed to live out their last, empty years with only the solace of a small pension.

And we are for a country where all of our people can work under labor standards that are fair and where responsible unionism is encouraged by laws that guarantee free collective bargaining.

We are for a country where we defend the liberties of all by defending the liberties of each, where the Bill of Rights and the Golden Rule are part of our being, where there is freedom to think, and to speak, and to doubt and dissent, and to be one's self.

We are for a country where no family's aspirations are bounded by unyielding barriers of race or of religious prejudice.

And these, my friends, are some of the things we have not yet fully achieved in this land. And because we have not there is among us a spiritual uneasiness, an empty feeling, a feeling that we have settled for too little, that we have accepted today's creature comforts at the price of the old ennobling dreams.

To see all these things is not to see failure, but only the job that still needs doing. America is well and strong above all nations of all time. We are the luckiest people in the world and we know it. To see these things, to roll up our sleeves, start doing something about them, is only to suggest, if you will, what we Democrats are for.

I talked of these things and of other matters recently to a beloved elder statesman of our party. How, I asked him, can all of these complexities be reduced to simple terms? He pointed out of the window to a man and woman and child walking down the street—a family any of you could count among your neighbors.

"Just ask yourself," he said, "who's looking out for those people, the ordinary people, down in Washington these days."

[At this point Mr. Stevenson's broadcast time expired. The rest of his speech follows.]

Well, there it is. Those people are not customers of our Government, they are owners, too.

The problem, and the Democratic answer to it, are as old as our party. Woodrow Wilson put it in these words:

I understand it to be the fundamental proposition of American liberty that we do not desire special privilege because we know special privilege will never comprehend the general welfare. This is the spiritual difference between adherents of the party now about to take charge of the Government and those who have been in charge of it in recent years.

We reassert tonight this simple yet essential faith—that democracy serves no one except as it serves us all.

EDUCATION

HOW DIFFERENT TYPES OF INSTITUTIONS
ARE PLANNING FOR THE FUTURE [1]

CORNELIS W. DE KIEWIET [2]

President Cornelis de Kiewiet, of the University of Rochester, gave this address on October 6, 1955, at the annual meeting of the American Council on Education, Mayflower Hotel, Washington, D.C.

The speaker moved at once into his theme: the problem of how to meet the forthcoming crisis of enlarged numbers and limited facilities in higher education. Two chief principles, according to the speaker, were to be kept in mind: (1) the "avoidance of rifts and controversy in the ranks of education itself;" and (2) the acceptance of the principle that "American higher education is held aloft on the two principles of both quality and quantity."

The address analyzed these problems with unusual originality and accompanying detail and concluded that "education is a form of statesmanship, that it serves the national interest in such a way that it is worth a high price in money and effort."

Dr. de Kiewiet's broad educational background and teaching experience were obvious at every turn in his message. His South African university studies, his doctorate at the University of London and further research at the universities of Paris and Berlin; his professorships in history at the State University of Iowa, and later at Cornell, where he also served as Dean of the College of Arts and Sciences, as provost, and as acting president; his more recent presidency of Rochester—all gave him historical insight and a thorough understanding of comparative higher education.

Critics of this address would challenge his selection of these problems of higher education. But few would question the cogency of his reasoning and the clearness with which he presented the issues.

The speaker's invention, disposition (organization), and style adhered to the classical rhetorical pattern. Impressive was the richness of vocabulary with here and there originality and force of phrasing. Dr. de Kiewiet is at home in extempore and animated delivery. His vocal inflection and pronunciation reflect his earlier British and continental associations.

[1] Text with permission for this reprint furnished through the courtesy of President Cornelis W. de Kiewiet.
[2] For biographical note, see Appendix.

It is the privilege of a speaker to take a topic such as has been assigned to me and adjust it to his own competence and interest. I could not draw up a detailed list of the schemes and plans now being considered by the numerous institutions of this country, nor am I sure that a mere catalog of experiments and expedients would be very clarifying. We could easily lose ourselves in a jungle of blueprints.

This is clearly a moment for the statement of general principles, for charting the main routes of our progress, and for surveying the major obstacles and pitfalls which lie ahead. As an individual I confess to some alternation in my own mind between hopefulness and fearfulness when I look at the interlocked problems of numbers, physical accommodation, financial needs and academic standards which we lump together in the clumsy phrase of the "coming student bulge."

In New York State alone very conservative estimates indicate that $750 million must be spent on physical plant alone in order to accommodate the increased enrollment of the next fifteen years. Educational leadership is under compulsion to pay the closest and most continuous attention to the manner in which these problems are discussed and understood by trustees, legislatures, civic leaders and their own faculties. Our first and major problem is the maintenance of understanding and of optimism. This is not a pleasant exhortation. It is an urgent and serious piece of advice. Education is in competition for financial support with other national needs which have powerful sponsorship. The bill for higher education will be presented after the states and communities have met the staggering bill for increased primary and secondary education. In the forthcoming White House Conference on Education the decision not to include higher education on the agenda for discussion indicates the priority that is being accorded to the problems of primary and secondary education.

An incident at the great meeting of the New York State branch of the White House Conference on Education was a portent of the pessimism and discouragement which higher education must plan to meet and overcome. The keynote speaker, General Royall, bluntly warned his audience that the burden of providing higher education for the great student populations of 1965 and 1970 might well be too great for society to meet. In consequence it might be necessary and wise to limit enrollment, and to accept the conclusion that our universities and colleges had fallen into the habit of admitting too many students who were not fitted for higher education.

This chilling gospel of austerity provoked many of the audience to anger or depression. Yet it served a most useful purpose. It was a warning that higher education must not assume that its case is already made. It was a warning that overstatement or exaggeration could provoke a pessimistic or defensive response. It was above all a warning that higher education cannot relax in the effort to convince its total constituency that its needs are realistic and in the national interest.

Most important in the first place is the avoidance of rifts and controversy in the ranks of education itself. A damaging and in my opinion useless controversy has raged about the manner in which the high school system of the country fails to provide adequate preparation for college and university. It is quite true that every college without exception has to take care of some unfinished high school business. It is quite true that the problems of numbers, costs and quality of instruction are made more difficult by this alleged defect or delinquency in secondary education. Somewhere we manage to lose at least a whole year, and maybe more, in the preparation of students who go on to college. But it is also true that in the system of secondary education in this country preparation for college is only one of many educational functions. It is not even the most important. The pattern of secondary education is set for our generation. The meaning of this is clear. The responsibility of dealing with the deficiencies of the high school graduate remains with the colleges and universities. It cannot be lessened by quarreling with the high schools, nor met by the premature and intemperate severity with which insufficient preparation is often punished in the first two years of college. If it is true that we are approaching a serious shortage in skilled and highly qualified manpower in the nation, then we cannot afford to flush out potential talent before it has had time to prove itself.

This is a familiar problem, provocative to conscientious faculties. But there are a number of important reasons for giving it a new and special prominence. There is an obvious trap into which some colleges and faculties seem already to have fallen. It is the trap of assuming that the total responsibilities of higher education can be met by a division of these responsibilities between colleges that are first-rate and those that are second-rate, or between private schools and public schools, between those who proudly take an uncompromising position on selectivity and standards, and those who cannot or do not want to do so. Some educators have been quite blunt in stating these assumptions publicly. In other cases these assumptions can be clearly read into pronouncements made in a more discreet or guarded fashion.

I have stepped into dangerous territory, and I know what objections and accusations I have exposed myself to. The contention is not that all institutions are equally good, which is manifestly absurd. Nor would it be sensible to suggest that there could be any simple formula for sharing the problems that will shortly beset us. The variety of our institutions and the diversity of their activities are the secret of strength and flexibility. The emphasis is upon a number of propositions. The first is upon the indivisibility of higher education, or upon the fact that a very real degree of cooperation is necessary if we are to reach the plateaus of 1965 and 1970 with an adequate and strengthened system of higher education. This cooperation will come more easily if there is a clearer understanding of the role of our diverse institutions. We have the task of explaining ourselves to one another. This is worth time and effort.

President Wriston tells a story about President Conant when he was about to assume office as President of Harvard. President Conant asked a distinguished educator for advice on which leading universities he might visit in order to become acquainted with the most advanced and creative effort in higher education. The question assumes that the answer would be some classic and ancient institution in Europe, or preferably close to Boston. But that was not the answer. The answer was the University of Chicago and the University of Minnesota. The story illus-

trates the important fact that in America there is no single traditional type of institution that sets a pattern for all others to
follow. American universities do not live in the shadow of a
few great institutions whose leadership and preeminence are
unquestioned. Some of the so-called Ivy League schools may
think they occupy such a place. It just is not so.

The reflective visitor to Great Britain will be impressed by
the vigor and growth of the municipal and provincial universities since the war. But he will also be impressed by the instinc-
tive acceptance of the greater stature and leadership of Oxford
and Cambridge. There is tacit acceptance of the sentiment of
the old music hall song: "Of course you could never be like us,
but be as like us as you're able to be." The serious trouble
British or French visitors always have in understanding university education in the United States results from their habit of
focusing upon a more traditional and uniform pattern. Even
Americans must be reminded that in this country the principle
prevails of "separate but equal" institutions.

We have the habit of evolving institutions to meet our
needs. The greater eastern institutions like Harvard, Yale and
Princeton were the adequate answer to the special educational
needs of the first generations of the nation. Roughly by the
time of the Civil War new needs had arisen for which both
additional and very different universities were required. It is
the task of the educational historian to tell the story of the new
needs in agriculture and technology, and of the greater numbers
of students for which the state universities made themselves
responsible. There is a story, too, of a season of secondariness
and an apparent dilution and debasement of educational objectives and standards. Some time after the turn of this century
(I would myself suggest after the first World War), the great
state universities had emerged as first line and adequate institutions which had transformed, enlarged and enriched the total
life of higher education, returning and exchanging men and
ideas on an equal level with the more ancient schools.

The conception that basic distinctions exist between private
and publicly supported schools must be replaced by a recognition that both have common objectives and carry joint responsi-

bilities. The consideration which the so-called private schools should give to the problems and opportunities of the publicly supported schools has a matching consideration on the other side. To be very specific, the problem of cooperation and coordination between these two types of schools in New York State is very delicate and difficult. The following extract from a report of a subcommittee of the New York State White House Conference on Education states the case excellently:

Historically in New York State the greatest proportion of the responsibility for higher education during many generations was borne by the private schools. Over the generations, plants were constructed, faculties assembled, and curricula established which now must be considered as an investment in higher education in New York which it is in the interest of the state to protect and indeed promote. It seems most essential that we refrain from accepting a traditional distinction between public and private education which placed them in opposite and incompatible categories. In other words, we cannot proceed effectively and constructively in answering forthcoming questions without insisting upon the essential indivisibility of higher education in the state. Where any estimate of the contributions which the private schools feel they can make to the coming problems of higher education falls short of what is considered as adequate or satisfactory, the only provisions must and should be made by the state. This area of state initiative is likely to be a wide one. The conclusion should not be immediately drawn that the inadequacies or insufficiencies can only be made up by the establishment of entirely new and so-called "public" institutions even though present knowledge and future study will undoubtedly disclose the fact that a number of new institutions will have to be called into being. Much ingenuity will doubtless be necessary to devise procedures which will be genuinely in the public interest and at the same time preserve the essential nature of existing institutions.

These comments are also the prologue to the future which now concerns us. We are entering a new period of growth and creativeness. Older institutions will grow and change. More significantly, new institutions will emerge and become the adequate answers to the needs of their generation. It is a reasonable prediction that right at this moment there are institutions in this country, as yet obscure or poor or small or struggling or immature, that a generation hence will be carrying much larger educational responsibilities. Of these, a few will probably be the third generation of those who have reached the plateaus of distinction and adequacy already reached by some of the great private and state universities. Some will be private and some will be public. Each one of us has a handful of front-running dark horses. Just as surely as after the founding of the land-grant institutions, there will be breaks with tradition, raised eyebrows and anxiety over the outcome of it all. Yet no institution, whatever its present stature, can in my judgment afford in its own or in the national interest to wrap itself around in its present habits and assumptions, and let others meet the challenge of the coming generation. What are burdens are also opportunities.

We must dispose, I believe, of another false contradiction which has entered the present national debate. It is a special form of the misleading distinction between institutions that are for the select few and those that must cater to the many. There is probably not a responsible faculty in the country which has not anxiously pondered the relationship between numbers of students and levels of instruction and training. In both graduate and undergraduate faculties an emphatic spokesmanship has arisen against sacrificing quality for quantity. Because this is a real fear, and because the cooperation and understanding of faculties are so essential, these doubts must be treated with respect, and be given satisfying answers.

The most significant difference between American higher education and British or French higher education is the acceptance in this country of a dual mandate. Since the Morrill Act of 1862, higher education, largely under the leadership of the state universities, accepted a responsibility for both numbers and quality. Since these words still suggest conflict and incompatibility, I would suggest that American higher education sets itself off against most other systems by most beneficially advancing the watershed of decision for a large proportion of the more able young men and women of the country. In this country a markedly higher proportion of the better minds is permitted to stay in the channels of education to a more mature age. This means more years for potential talent to reveal itself, an increased sense of personal participation in the major decisions of life, and a greater awareness of the wide range of choices that can be made.

The true greatness of American higher education is held aloft on the two pillars of both quality and quantity. What is sometimes referred to disparagingly as mass education has been compatible with the emergence of graduate, technical and professional schools that are brilliant in any company. We can do ourselves immense harm by not continuing this dual mandate. There is already manifest in this country a sort of flight from the undergraduate. It is a complex phenomenon, and it is not easy to be fair in describing it. It is a movement from the undergraduate college to the graduate school, from general education to specialization, from teaching to research, from the student as a whole to the student as a potential graduate or advanced professional student, from the large lecture room to the small seminar, from the many again to the few. Of course, this is not an indictment of research or specialization or the desire to provide the best in scholarship. Our need for these is still greater than we can yet satisfy. But there is nonetheless room for an urgent reminder that it is most emphatically not in the national interest to lessen the proportion of those who go to college, to try to thrust back into the high schools tasks we should carry out ourselves, or to be less solicitous of the broad needs of the undergraduate population of universities and colleges.

If the correction is made for the differences in national population, ten times as many American boys and girls go to college as in Great Britain. What this means is not that ten times as many American boys and girls get a good education. But it does mean that a far higher proportion of America's youth are given until they are twenty or twenty-one before they need to decide what to do with their lives. In Great Britain this choice for the bulk of the nation's youth is made at best five years earlier, and often earlier still. It would be most difficult to exaggerate the great national significance of this fact. In the United States a far smaller proportion of young men and women need feel that some arbitrary social, economic or academic decision was imposed upon them at an immature age, so that they had no real share in the selection of their walk of life. By the same token a far higher proportion can legitimately feel that their society has permitted them to defer the critical decision of a career until through age, knowledge and experience, they are likely to make it wisely and in accordance with their own wishes. Young people who have had this advantage are less likely to feel that their society has dealt harshly with them, less likely to become members of dissident groups inspired by a special sense of grievance and denial. It is a fair conclusion that this sense of grievance and denial has contributed to the dissension and tension which mark the attitude of some of the French political parties.

To the American observer there is something missing in the attitude of Great Britain's industry and British universities to technological education. What is missing is the acceptance by universities of a proper responsibility to help in the training of the student of good but not first-class ability. The ordinary American graduate, not the first-class man who is headed for the top professions, but the rank-and-file student, is the foundation on which American industry is built. The poor support given to American universities by American industry is an indication that industry itself does not recognize this fact. Nonetheless, the run-of-the-mine student, who would have little chance of being accepted in a French or British university, acquires a literateness in science, and an awareness in political and economic issues, a receptiveness in technological affairs, that in their sum total are an incalculable national asset. It is difficult to estimate the support, cooperation and sympathy which our first-rate scientists, engineers and other professional men get from the high percentage of college men amongst their subordinates and assistants.

For want of a really widespread scientific and technological literateness Great Britain, like France, pays a heavy price impossible to estimate. British colonial administrators are the best in the world save in this one respect. Apart from the great and brilliant engineers who served the imperial cause in India, Egypt and elsewhere, it is unhappily true that the most pervasive defect of the British colonial servant is an unawareness of science and technology that hides from him often simple solutions of some of his administrative problems. The most obvious shortage in French and British industry is in the cadres of management and technical personnel which in America are commonly recruited from the universities. The most obvious blind spot is the failure of industrial leaders to recognize that an increase in these cadres would pay dividends in initiative, ideas, daring, innovation and the other qualities that set off American from European industry. As it is, men of spirit tend to concentrate below the level of management and technological leadership, often in a posture of resentment. Thus potential abilities capable of stimulating the economy become inert and indifferent, or at worst a drag upon progress, as a result of economic or social antagonism. The delinquency of industry and education in Great Britain and France consists in not recognizing that the loss in the First World War alone of 800,000 dead in Great Britain and nearly 2 million in France called for a special effort to recruit in the mass of the population the talent and ability that were lost in Flanders. American industry has a debt to our universities not generally enough recognized for their contribution to the reservoir of trained men, for assistance in removing class tensions, and for creating the pervading sense of opportunity of American economic and social life.

It is very clear that France pays a heavy price for its educational achievements, superb though they often are. For financial reasons alone it is certain that a serious proportion of potentially first-class young men never get started. The greatest beneficiary of American education, the man who is second class, but perfectly capable of acquiring a sound command of some skill, suffers even more drastically. It is impossible to measure the sum total of disappointment and frustration that is produced in the narrowing channel that leads to higher education in France. It is a little easier at least to guess at the damage done in industry, government, and elsewhere because of the insufficent flow of people trained to the limit of their capacity. The demands of the welfare state, of science and technology, of rehabilitation, throw too much responsibility for leadership and decision upon too few people. There can be no doubt at all that the indecencies of French politics are related to the lower proportion of university men in politics and the constituencies. Before the Second World War there was at least one Minister of Finance who did not know the rudiments of tax collection, not to speak of money and banking. Flandin never read a serious book, and yet spoke for France on momentous occasions. If there is not a serious Communist party in the United States, as there is in France, American education can claim a share in the benefit, since at no point in the American educational system is a boy made seriously to feel that for want of educational opportunity, he cannot hope to find a place in society suited to his talents. The American system of education from top to bottom is the costliest in the world. It is wasteful of time and money, but as a great solvent which smooths out incompatible social differences, and as a principal architect of national coherence, time and money have been cheap prices to pay. To a greater extent than in Great Britain or France popular education in the United States has been a force working for social cooperation, and for the mitigation of those drastic conflicts in political life which divide class from class and sometimes end in collapse or revolution. The continued successful extension of the two great political parties in America, including the major social and economic groups of the nation, while communism has split and weakened the liberal parties of France, and socialism has driven out the British Liberal party, is genuinely owing to a system of American education which has sought to leave behind separations and snobberies. The sharp social cleavage in Great Britain which education rather maintains than seeks to eliminate undeniably did much to eliminate the Liberal party and substitute for it the class conscious Labour party.

Whenever legislatures balk on appropriations, or trustees call special sessions on the budget, or corporations try to get away with token contributions, or faculties shy at the magnitude of our obligations, here surely is the correct answer, that education is a form of statesmanship, that it serves the national interest in such a way that it is worth a high price in money and effort.

THE IMPORTANCE OF BEING AN INDIVIDUAL [3]

HAROLD W. DODDS [4]

President Harold W. Dodds gave this baccalaureate address to the class of 1955, before some 2,500 students and their friends on June 12, 1955, in the Princeton University chapel.

The President's theme, that of the contemporary "bigness" and the threats to individuality, was a major issue on almost every campus. The trends, since the two world wars, had been toward group association and conformity. This trend was accelerated by the wider social movement as well as by the accelerated expansion of our political and industrial civilization.

Educators, including Presidents Virgil Hancher of Iowa State University, Grayson Kirk of Columbia, and Nathan Pusey of Harvard, had protested against the drift toward standardization of thinking and conduct. Dr. Dodds, "one of the foremost authorities on local government problems," stressed again in this address the historic philosophy of individualism as expounded by Ralph Waldo Emerson in his Harvard address on the American scholar. But the Princeton president thought and talked in the context of 1955-1956 with his analysis of the problem of all educated men who would both preserve their personal character and discharge their social-political-economic responsibilities in this complicated world.

Dr. Dodds' solution was for the graduate to think of "self realization in terms of richer aspirations than preoccupation with material goods and services." He would point again, as American educational leaders have done, to sound education as grounded in the concept of individual worth—that worth embodied in our Hebraic-Hellenic religious ideals.

Although not a dynamic orator, President Dodds has commanded long educational leadership through the force of his ideas and his communicative directness.

My topic this morning is the importance of being an individual. It is a subject which recurs repeatedly in student discussions on our campus. As a rule they open by someone making the accusation that to succeed here an undergraduate must conform to a certain pattern, usually referred to as the Princeton type. It is the easy-going good guys with a strong

[3] The text and permission for this reprint furnished through the courtesy of President Harold W. Dodds.

[4] For biographical note, see Appendix.

ingredient of party Charlies who set the tone of the place, it is charged. Certain ignoble adjectives are sometimes invoked to describe further the imputed stereotype such as complacent, apathetic, anti-intellectual, blasé, smooth, urbane. The inclination of undergraduates to dress alike is cited to drive home the point; although I must interpolate that if this is an evil it is not peculiar to Princeton. Ivy League slacks with contrasting sports jackets are practically a national institution among American colleges for those occasions where khaki pants, a sweat shirt and soiled buckskin shoes do not suffice. At a university which I once served the uniform was soiled corduroy trousers and autographed felt hats, but the principle was the same. In any event, the charge is that individuality is smothered under a hard crust of campus customs and frozen standards of behavior, and that whoever seeks to break through the crust does so at his peril. The safest and surest way to be a campus success is to conform.

The matter was the subject of a searching editorial last winter in the *Daily Princetonian.* The writer recognized that pressures to conform to exist here and that an uncritical and facile conformity often pays rewards of a sort. But he went on to observe, I think rightfully, that although some "may sacrifice intellectual integrity and true individuality to what they conceive of as a stereotype," students are in error "when they think that a good life at Princeton entails such sacrifice;" and he concluded that success here "is a problem which each individual must solve for himself." I congratulate the author of the editorial for his ability to lift the subject out of a purely local undergraduate context to the broader aspects of life in general.

If the question of conformity versus nonconformity were a subject only of Princeton campus concern, I should not be talking about it to you, who on Tuesday will say goodbye to your undergraduate days forever. If you feel that your student years have been a frustrating struggle against an unwholesome social stereotype, wait until you come under the pressures of business and professional life. You will find that to be an individual then will require more intelligence and courage than in a university which of all places in the world is most hospitable to dissenters and to differences of tastes and opinion.

Nevertheless, however heavy may be the pressures urging you to conform here or elsewhere, if you have the makings of a genuine individual you will discover that no matter how hard you try to rationalize surrender to them, you will not succeed save at the loss of the greatest asset you possess, your self-respect. The divine urge to be an individual, the real man's resistance to being a rubber stamp even if being one pays off in short-term satisfactions, will keep cropping up to disturb your peace of mind. The reason lies very deep in human nature.

In the current fictional *Memoirs of Hadrian,* which some of you undoubtedly have read, the emperor is made to say, "A part of every life, even a life meriting very little regard, is spent in searching out the reasons for its existence, its starting point and its source." If the emperor was right, and I think he was, no man will find the answer except in himself as an individual; it is not a question which he can refer for decision to any external authority or group; no counselor or priest can settle it for him. He will find the answer as to why he is here on earth, what he should be doing while he is here, and where he is going hereafter only within himself.

Of course, being an individual does not mean that one has no responsibilities to society, that one's obligation is only to his own self-indulgent happiness and well-being. Being an individual is the antithesis of every man for himself and the devil catch the hindermost. True, every human being has a life of his own to live and an individuality to preserve and nourish, but this does not support the philosophy of the elephant that chanted as he danced among the chickens, "each for himself and God for all of us."

Nor can one become an individual just by being queer. Some undertake to fulfill themselves by cultivating eccentricity; but unless they are authentic geniuses—not merely self-appointed ones—they are apt to wind up by being merely pathetic. To be an individual, one must not be afraid of being different, but difference for the sake of difference does not make a man.

When one starts to study the anatomy of individuality, the first thing that strikes one's attention is that not all conformity is bad; on the contrary, man must practice a large degree of conformity, else individuals would have no chance to develop at all. Our society would fly apart as a result of its own centrifugal forces did we not conform willingly to many prevailing social patterns and habits. For example, unless one is under the clearest compulsion of conscience to act otherwise, it is one's duty to observe the law of the land, particularly in a democracy in which the people make the laws and retain the power to change them by peaceful means. Moreover, there is another vast field of conduct quite outside legal commandments and regulations, which involves what has been termed "obedience to the unenforceable." It refers to those broad essentials of personal behavior which no civil or penal laws reach, but which civilized people are bound to observe. Being a good neighbor, sensitive to your civic responsibilities, is one instance of the duty we owe to obey the unenforceable. Good manners is another. I don't mean just the etiquette of the drawing room. Many a man practices good manners in the truest sense who knows little about how to handle a teacup or how he should arrange his knife and fork on his dinner plate. Fundamentally, good manners are the embodiment of one's moral respect and consideration for others.

The commendable desire to be oneself must also envisage one's duty to the organizations of which one is a part. One can be a good team player and a constructive individual as well. Up to a point, you will find it your duty to adjust yourself to the good of the business organization for which you work, the partnership of which you are a member or the neighborhood in which you live. Note, however, my "up to a point" qualification, for occasions do arise in which it is your obligation not to conform. One great evil of the Nazi and Communist philosophies is that they omit this "up to a point" qualification and demand the complete subordination of the individual to the system. Any system that follows this line carries the germs of its own ultimate destruction.

But there is perhaps a greater threat to individuality than either fascism or communism. It is the big scale on which modern life is organized. This is the day of big business, big cities, big governments, big labor unions, big politics, which involve a way of life so unlike that of the simple handicraft economy in which our ancestors lived and worked. "Everything," we are told in tones of considerable despair, "is getting bigger except the individual, and he is getting smaller and more insignificant and dependent on large social units."

You recognize this as a familiar indictment of the times. If it is true, the future of the individual man is dark indeed, and in urging you to cultivate a healthy independence of judgment I am wasting my breath. Is it true, however, that our complex society necessarily depersonalizes people, while enriching them in respect to material goods? Is the individual really becoming expendable, a production number or a mere fractional particle in a table of statistics, engulfed in a world of soulless corporations, chain stores, chain newspapers, national advertising, mass communication and mass indoctrination through radio, movies and television? Is the individual man going the way of the buffalo?

This I do not believe and I challenge the proposition that, to paraphrase the words of a recent critic, our society has become so impersonal that people really need their initials on the cover of their toilet cases to "remind them who they are."

It is true that, measured in terms of raising one's own food, weaving one's own cloth, cutting one's own firewood, molding one's own candles, managing one's own country store or blacksmith shop, or being one's own doctor, it does seem that a man has less range in which to operate as an individual than he used to have. But are these the right tests to apply in searching for the answer to our question? Is there not another side to the picture? Is it not true that our complex economy, in releasing us from the necessity to weave our own cloth or make our own candles, has also released us from many crushing elemental anxieties and long exhausting hours of manual labor which characterized the handicraft economy? Were not our individualistic ancestors in many respects more regimented, more tied to the wheel than we are? By comparison the average man today enjoys an unparalleled opportunity for new high levels of satisfactions, now that so much of his time and strength is no longer consumed in merely subsisting. Need the dignity of man suffer because as a worker he must function in coordination with larger groups? On the contrary, has not the ever increasing productiveness of our economy given us the opportunity for a life less earth-bound than we ever enjoyed before? Is not industry learning rapidly that its employees are not a labor commodity but self-respecting individuals? Is it not true that the more complex, the more highly organized our society becomes, the more it requires competent, self-respecting individuals to make it work? Are not the most advanced societies those in which you will find the individuals most highly developed? No, I do not see that mankind is being returned to the level of ants and bees. On the contrary, I see hopeful signs that he is moving the other way.

What I suggest to you is that the large-scale basis of life today, with all its difficult problems of mass opinion and mass organization, is really an opportunity for greater self-realization rather than less. So I conclude that, no matter how much one may yearn sentimentally for a return to the simple life of the past, no man who has had access to a good education can today rationalize his failure to be a person on the grounds that the massive scale of life restricts the scope of the individual. What we moderns must do is to think of self-development in terms of richer aspirations than preoccupation with the production of material goods and services. Surely we can standardize automobiles without standardizing the higher reaches of the mind. Surely the fact that many of us can own automobiles today, who would not have been able to support a horse and buggy fifty years ago, should enable us to strengthen rather than force us to diminish our uniquely human qualities of personality.

The movement of Western civilization has been marked by expanding freedom from the rule of rigid custom, ritual and status towards greater stress on the worth of the individual and a larger tolerance and respect for the man who deviates. Science with its curiosity to discern new knowledge has made a profound contribution to freeing man's soul from bondage to caste and unchallenged tradition. The long history of the idea of civil rights, the right to freedom of religion, freedom of opinion, and freedom of speech, the philosophy underlying the Fifth Amendment, reveal successive steps towards realization of the worth of the human soul, one's own soul, and the souls of others. What the poets and preachers tell us about the unique individual with all his enduring personal hopes and fears, aspirations, ambitions and responsibilities for self-realization is true.

In all ages the easiest course has been to let one's environment mold him. It requires an energetic spirit and a strong will to express oneself under any circumstances. Thornton Wilder has written of the "loneliness that accompanies independence and the uneasiness that accompanies freedom." The danger today is not so much that the world will force you to conform, as it is that you will want to conform; that you will prefer not to be the master of your fate, the captain of your soul. As Mr. Justice Brandeis is said to have remarked, "The irresistible is often only that which is not resisted."

Life's toughest decisions are in this area. There is no mathematical formula by which you can settle the problem of what you will be and what you will stand for. As the *Princetonian* editor expressed it, it is a problem which everyone must solve for himself. How you decide relates to your sensitivity to human values, to your allegiance to those unique qualities of the spirit which mark mankind off from even the highest animals.

In conclusion, may I relate what I have been saying to the nature of these baccalaureate exercises, which traditionally take the form of a religious service in our chapel, dedicated to the abiding truths of our faith. It is our belief that God is daily manifesting himself in us, his creatures and his children, that validates our worth and glory as individuals with a peculiar destiny of our own. It is our personal relationship to a supernatural being which sets "an absolute value on the dignity of every human being." St. Paul tells us not to be conformed to this world but to be transformed that we "may prove what is the good and acceptable and perfect will of God." As our faith supports the integrity and autonomy of the individual, so does it impose the grave but noble obligation to be one. That divine thirst for some purpose and permanence to our existence as autonomous individuals, the universal search to which the Roman

Emperor Hadrian referred, summons us to obedience to a personal being outside ourselves and yet an integral part of us as
individuals; and in response to this summons we find fulfillment.

There are a good many influences these days, more than I
have time to mention, which can readily lead a man to assume
that the coverage which it takes to face the loneliness and unease
of being oneself represents but a futile gesture against over-
whelming forces.

Now that astronomy has shown us that man is physically less
than a speck in an immeasurable universe; now that our big society is modifying the social relations of the individual to others;
now that we know more about the influence of social trends on
conduct, more about the play of unconscious psychological incentives and more about the chemistry of the brain, man's erstwhile
purely rational view of himself has suffered some sharp shocks.
But the self-conscious human being has survived, and, I promise
you, will continue to survive. The more science can tell us about
the natural aspects of our world and of ourselves, the more will
our human and spiritual energies be released to express themselves. Science and technology do not diminish personality, unless
we want it that way.

In moving poetic language the composer of the Eighth Psalm
summarizes all and more than I have said this morning. First,
he refers to the question which I have just mentioned and which
no thoughtful person can escape: Is not the individual man too
minute a particle in vast space, or as we might say in this modern
age of social science, too small an element in a gigantic determined social mechanism, to be of any significance in himself?
The Psalmist puts the question to the Lord in this way:

> When I consider thy heavens, the work of thy fingers,
> The moon and the stars, which thou hast ordained;
> What is man, that thou art mindful of him?
> And the son of man, that thou visitest him?

It is, I repeat, a natural question for us moderns, as it was for
the Psalmist. But he wavers only for a moment; promptly he

goes on to reassure us regarding man's sovereign place in all creation in the memorable sentences:

> For thou hast made him a little lower than the angels,
> And hast crowned him with glory and honor.
> Thou madest him to have domininon over the works of
> thy hands;
> Thou hast put all things under his feet.

If you remember this through all the years to come you will not be seduced into depersonalizing conformity; you will be an individual. I commend it, not as a man learned in theology or the doctrines of the church, but as an ordinary citizen who has found that this faith is both rational and practical. It is a mystery, I know, but so in the deepest sense is tomorrow's sunrise or the prospect that you will be graduated on Tuesday.

RELIGION

THE VISION OF FAITH [1]

PATRICK A. O'BOYLE [2]

His Excellency, Patrick A. O'Boyle, Archbishop of Washington, gave this Reparation Day sermon on January 1, 1956, at the St. Matthew's Cathedral, Washington, D.C. The day was dedicated to prayer for persecuted Catholics throughout the world.

The theme was a direct criticism of the United States because it has been "outmaneuvered and outgunned by the Communists in the very area where our strength should be greatest—the area of ideals."

The discourse was highly persuasive. Its pattern consisted of a vigorous and specific analysis of the present situation—in which communism continued its persecution of religions and Christian leaders; in which the United States was too completely concentrating on military, economic and political opposition to the Iron Curtain countries, but neglecting our supreme weapon—Christian idealism. The speaker's solution, "the action step," called not only for prayers and penance, but for a strong and continuous "speaking out," through lay organizations as well as through government agencies, to expose the real nature of communism. This pattern of persuasion was accompanied by refutation of those American attitudes based upon apathy or aloofness. The speaker's language was filled with rhetorical questions and similar persuasive elements.

In logical development of the theme, concreteness of illustration and citations, in vigor of style and delivery, the sermon was one of the most impressive of the year.

Be on the watch, stand fast in the faith, be full of courage—*I Corinthians, 16:13-16.*

Last week you may have seen in the newspapers the pictures of two medical missionaries released from Communist China. I can still see the emaciated features, the dull, staring eyes

[1] The text is from the *Catholic Standard*. 6:13. January 6, 1956. Permission for this reprint through the cooperation and courtesy of the Most Reverend Archbishop of Washington, D.C., Patrick A. O'Boyle. The sermon was also reprinted in the *Congressional Record* 102:(daily) A302-3. January 16, 1956.

[2] For biographical note, see Appendix.

telling of agonies that are beyond our power to imagine. These kindly souls had left America on a mission of Christian mercy. They went thousands of miles overseas to a country that was strange in language, customs, and outlook on life. They took this journey as a gesture of faith, bringing religious truth as they saw it to those who knew not Christ.

Now they are coming home, broken in body and wounded in spirit. They gave kindness; in return they were imprisoned. They sought to win the souls of men; they were accused of being agents of a foreign political power. Their mission was one of mercy and healing; their reward was a charge of treason. Surely we see in this story a capsule picture of the challenge that our age faces. When mercy is considered treason, truth is classed as a lie, and good is called evil, we are indeed faced with a monstrous perversion of human nature, a denial of every ideal that civilized man has cherished.

On this Sunday, dedicated as a day of reparation for the evils caused by godless communism, it is fitting that we examine once again the bitter realities of our time. What happened to the two kindly souls released last week is not an isolated incident. Over a billion human beings, our brothers and sisters under God, are in danger of a similar fate.

We must never forget the names of Cardinals Mindszenty, Stepinac, and Wyszynski, of Archbishop Beran, and of our own Bishop Byrne of Washington and Bishop Ford of New York, and of thousands of other bishops and priests, religious and lay people, too numerous to list here. We should never overlook the millions of silent martyrs, some slain, others imprisoned or sent to slave labor camps—all because they believed in God and stood steadfast for their religion. When we think of these sufferings, we should be shocked by the prancing and posturing of Communist leaders as they tour the world, receiving heroes' welcomes. What has happened to the world today when such monstrous evils are so easily forgotten and so readily overlooked?

The leaders of the Communist world are not trying to deceive us in regard to their attitude toward religion. They state openly that the conflict with religious faith is a war to death. They are cynical enough to practice some toleration at certain times, to cultivate some church leaders while persecuting others, and even to seek to use religion as a tool for imperialist gains. But they do not hide their long-range plans. Those who are deceived about the essential conflict between communism and religion are self-deceived.

I think that most of my fellow Americans will agree with this analysis of the true nature of communism. Yet it is possible that some may think that this is no concern of ours. They may express their views in this way: We grant that it is deplorable that hundreds of millions have been deprived of their basic human rights under this evil system. It is indeed tragic that churches have been closed, the clergy exiled or imprisoned, the teaching of religion prohibited, and even private practice of religion made dangerous and akin to treason. We do not condone these evils, but at the same time it is not our mission to right all the wrongs in the world. We may reject the racism of the Union of South Africa, but as a nation we must admit that it is the internal problem of another sovereign power. We know that economic injustice prevails in many areas of the world. Yet we dare not tell other countries how to manage their own economies. So likewise we must consider the civil liberties of Communist subjects as an internal problem of these regimes.

Now such persons would not contend that communism is not a problem for Americans. But they visualize the problem in terms of economic, military, and political factors. Our proper concern, they say, is only with matters of our own national security. We trespass beyond this field at our peril. Meddling nations, no matter what their good intentions, are greeted with resentment and often with contempt by fellow sovereign powers. Indeed, one analyst, formerly high in the councils of our nation, considers the "moralizing trend" one of the great weaknesses of American diplomacy.

It is not my intention to comment from the pulpit on matters of diplomacy or to seek to define the proper scope of political action. Rather than discuss these issues here, we might accept for the moment the idea that national security is our only proper concern in dealing with other nations. Even with this concession, it is still not true that we must consider only the economic, military, and political menace of communism. To look at the struggle in these narrow terms is to miss the real conflict of our day. The real war today has well been described as a war for the minds of men. It is a clash of beliefs, of allegiances, and, in a certain sense, of ideals. The use of the term "ideal" in reference to communism may seem strange. Yet such a keen observer as the late Pope Pius XI did not hesitate to say that

the Communist idea wins over many of the better-minded members of the community. . . .

We have noted before how timely is the analysis of communism written by this great Pontiff. Although the document is nearly twenty years old, it can still be read with immense profit today. And one of its finest features is the study of the appeal of communism in terms of idealism. The Pope noted some of the arguments of the Communists in regard to social reforms. He then stated:

And as every error contains its element of truth, the partial truths to which we have referred are astutely presented according to the needs of time and place, to conceal, when convenient, the repulsive crudity and inhumanity of Communist principles and tactics. . . . The preachers of communism are also proficient in exploiting racial antagonisms and political divisions and oppositions. They take advantage of the lack of orientation characteristics of modern agnostic science in order to burrow into the universities where they bolster up the principles of their doctrine with pseudo-scientific arguments. [Both quotations from "On Atheistic Communism," March 19, 1937, No. 15]

Although these words were written nearly twenty years ago, they could be a description of Communist tactics today in great nations of Asia, Europe, Africa, and Latin America. We must remember that the appeal of communism is not only to the disgruntled, the bitter, and the neurotic members of a community. It has been able to convince men of sensitive natures and of high ideals. The world was shocked when spy rings were uncovered in our own country, in Canada, in Great Britain, and in Australia—not only because of the gravity of the secrets betrayed, but also because of the respectable nature of those who preferred communism to their own country. These men were scientists, university professors, and others of real standing in their communities.

The process of winning over misguided idealists still continues. And it is far more dangerous to the security of the world than most of us realize. Our country is inclined to underestimate the power of the intellectual. We call such persons egg-heads, or ivory tower professors. But in the brains of such scientists was born the fearful weapons of modern war—the ultimate weapons of fission and fusion. In wide areas of the world, men of learning are the real leaders of their nations. This is particularly true in nations newly freed from colonial status. It is in these very areas that the power of communism is growing with sobering speed.

By concentrating almost exclusively on the economic, military, and political menace of communism, we have been able to counter its threats of this type. We have reached a stalemate, with the result that our fears of war have lessened. Yet at the same time we feel that somehow we are losing in the struggle with the Communist world. While we patch a leak here and a trickle there, a flood wave of sympathy for communism is sweeping many parts of Asia and Africa. We are baffled and bewildered as our best efforts seem to fail.

Could it be that we are failing because we have conceived the struggle too narrowly? Are we fighting with nineteenth-century weapons of diplomacy a twentieth-century battle of ideology? Do we talk in terms of material wealth and military power, while our opponents monopolize the powerful slogans of justice, of peace, and of equality? Are we addicted to showing power, letting the Communists speak of ideals? The answer to all these questions, I fear, is yes. And therein lies the secret of our frustration today. We are out-maneuvered and outgunned in the very area where our strength should be the greatest. By default, we have permitted the enemy to use our choicest weapons.

If the real war today is the struggle for men's minds, we need badly an agonizing reappraisal of our policy and tactics. We face a total conflict between two ways of life. In such a conflict, the old distinctions between the internal policy of a nation and its foreign conduct are completely unreal. The leaders of communism are offering a total package. It is true that their advertising is deceptive. The contents of the package are quite different from the promises of the label. But, in this case, by the time that the purchaser knows the truth, it is usually too late. He can no longer return the package and regain his freedom.

What must be our policy in this struggle? It seems simple enough—to tell the whole truth again and again about communism and compare it with the whole truth again and again about the free world. Yet it is not so simple as it seems. Why? Because we have not yet dared, as a people, to speak frankly and openly the truth about communism. We do not hesitate to build a powerful army, navy, and air force. We have ringed the world with alliances, formed for the sole purpose of containing the Communist orbit. We spend millions for propaganda. Yet, at the same time, we are strangely quiet about the purpose of all these activities. We engage in a form of pretense, as if it were not proper to mention the subject of communism in polite company.

Pussyfooting on such issues plays directly into the hands of the enemy. They utter their lies bluntly and fearlessly, while we leave the truth muted and gagged. Let me return to the story I told you at the beginning of this discourse. The peoples of the world are deeply religious. They respect the mercy and humanity of the medical profession. Most of them acknowledge and respect the basic rights of man. Yet all these ideals are trampled into the dust by communism, and we treat it as a private affair.

Have we lost our sense of indignation? Are we so self-satisfied, so complacent, so preoccupied with enjoying our ever-mounting standards of living that we blind ourselves to cruelty and bitter slavery visited upon our fellow man? Is this the America that fought for the ideals of freedom and independence in 1776, the nation that endured the war between the states, the people who generously responded in the recent World War when millions died to overthrow the tyranny of a Hitler? Have we been hypnotized into a moral slumber? Let us all examine our consciences and face our duty honestly and openly.

Please do not misunderstand me. I am not pleading that we use religion, or medicine, or law as propaganda weapons in a political struggle. We do not ask governments to speak for the Church or the medical or legal professions. But I do believe that the American people should speak out, through their proper organizations and representatives, on the real nature of communism. We should realize that the struggle is total, and not merely a matter for governmental action only. And our political authorities in turn can report, in a proper way, the sentiments of the American people.

Permit me to give an example of the leader of a great organization facing up to the challenge of the day and speaking his mind on Communist activities. George Meany, President of the AFL-CIO, addressing the National Religion and Labor Foundation in New York, on December 13, did not hesitate to picture vividly the heartless inhumanity of the slave labor camps and the depths of degradation to which Communist brutalities have brought the opponents of the Soviet system. We need more Americans to speak openly, fearlessly and honestly the truth, the whole truth without any apology.

But there is another side to the picture. If we ask the uncommitted peoples of the world to choose between our way of life and life under communism, we must be sure that we can stand the comparison. It is easy to say that the Communists are out and out materialists and that we honor God and respect our fellow man. But are we prepared to prove our point? Suppose that the charge is made that our films show that we are a degraded and sensual people. What if we are portrayed as money-mad, seeking only material comforts and wealth, and blind to the riches of the spirit? Have we an answer if a visitor who differs from us in race is subject to insults because of the color of his skin? Can we say for sure that others regard us as more idealistic than the Communists? Unfortunately, the answer is that many peoples think that there is little choice between the two systems.

Today, then, as in our Christian charity we pray for the victims of communism, let us dedicate ourselves to a total struggle to help our bruised and wounded fellow men, lying by the roadside. First, let us storm the gates of heaven with prayer and with penance, asking that God give them strength to endure their persecution, and that the day of deliverance be not too far off.

In the spirit of our Saviour, let us also pray for the persecutors. Today their hearts are blackened with hate. May God give them the light to see the truth, and the grace to love their fellow man. Let us make this prayer a definite and regular part of our lives, so that we will not forget our brethren in need. We should not overlook the other powerful spiritual weapon: penance. Let us gladly embrace the sacrifice involved in living blameless lives. In addition, we might at some set time, perhaps once a week, offer to the Almighty some real act of penance and reparation—giving up something that pleases us, or offering our help to some unfortunate person. Here is something that each of us can do, no matter what may be our positions in life.

At the same time, let us not neglect the human means that God has put at our disposal. Above all, we should speak out fearlessly and portray the struggle for men's minds in its true terms. It is more than the political or the military or the economic. It is a struggle between those who acknowledge God and reverence His name, and as a consequence respect the rights of their fellow man—and those who deny God and despise man. But if we presume to fight under the banners of the Almighty, let us be worthy of this honor. May our lives and conduct shine from the vision of faith. Truth is great, and it shall prevail. May this truth be in us and in our actions, so that we may be instruments in the hands of God, shaped to bring peace and justice in the world once again. Stand fast in the faith, be full of courage and let everything you do, be done in a spirit of charity.

MAKING A NEW START [3]

NATHAN A. PERILMAN [4]

Rabbi Nathan Perilman, of Congregation Emanu-El, Fifth Avenue at Sixty-fifth Street, New York City, gave this sermon marking the Jewish New Year (Rosh Hashanah) on September 27, 1954.

Keynote of this ten-day holiday is "the belief that human nature can be improved by the application of divine ideals to daily life. Religious services on the holiday stress the theme of the possibility of overcoming weaknesses and faults. This idea is embodied in prayers, preachment, and liturgy."

Rabbi Perilman received his elementary education in the schools of Ohio, and his bachelor's degree at the University of Pittsburgh, in 1926. His speech training consisted largely of the practical business of debating in high school and university. [5]

At Pittsburgh he was elected to Delta Sigma Rho, honorary forensic society, for his superior intercollegiate debating. His rabbinical training he completed at the Hebrew Union College, Cincinnati, in 1932. For the past twenty-four years he has been in wide demand and has steadily grown as a speaker, and, whimsically, he admits that he "has done an endless amount of speaking—some think too much."

The sermon printed below reflects the breadth of his Judaic theology and philosophy, with its practical application to the problem of contemporary communism and other currents that affect the American ideals of tolerance, cooperative living, and outlook.

Nothing so unmans us or destroys our hope or reduces us to despair, as the realization that we have come to the end of our strivings. When we are told that nothing more can be done, no new steps can be taken, that there are no new remedies to try, we are reduced to frustration and helplessness. A man needs to be able to make a new start. Dead ends, stone walls, iron curtains violate our sense of the order of the universe. It is as though we are lifted off the sure ground on which alone we can stand, as if the laws of gravity have been abrogated; for in a universe in which there is constant change and motion, a

---

[3] Text supplied through the courtesy of Rabbi Morris Kertzer, of the American Jewish Committee, and Rabbi Nathan Perilman.

[4] For biographical note, see Appendix.

[5] Letter to this editor, November 9, 1955.

human being must be able to make a new start, find a new point of beginning and try again.

This is the miracle and the essence and the heart of this holy season which is now beginning. Long centuries ago our forefathers with a peculiar prescience into the compulsions of human being saw the necessity for interrupting the steady flow of daily life for a little time so that mankind could look at themselves, review themselves, and renew themselves. The holy season was not intended as a vacation from life. It was not an escape from reality. Our forefathers were the supreme realists. As such, they had a high regard for spiritual values and spiritual wholesomeness. When this period of soul searching was over, when they were reconciled and ready to begin again, they went back eagerly to the business of living. This has not been a time of escape, of lightness or gaiety. It has always been a serious time. New starts and spiritual renewal are not won merely by presenting one's self at the door of the sanctuary nor through the kindly intercession of a temple functionary. This calls for earnest self-searching, honest self-appraisal and a whole-hearted resolve to begin again in a new and better way.

When a person starts afresh, even with the newness of a new day, or the stimulus of altered circumstances, or with the inspiration of a new outlook upon life, he refreshes the deepest principles by which he lives. It is sad indeed, when a man must believe that today must inevitably be like yesterday and tomorrow can only be like today. Even when we live in an age such as the one through which we are passing of constant and unrelieved crisis, we need a holy season like this to break the monotony of our uncertainty. There is a human instinct which tells us that our life which is meant to have order and unity and continuity, is no less meant to be full of new beginnings and new starts and new hopes, and new opportunities. The human spirit needs ever to be renewing its forces in order to begin again. It is to think on these things that this holy season is given to us.

When we reflect deeply and honestly upon our age; when we get past the point of partisanship, even the wholesome kind of partisanship; when we get beyond the vexatious business of personalities and groups who seem bent on spoiling our happiness and destroying our way of life; when we get to the very heart of the sickness of our time which with all of our wonderful resources we are not able to understand, we usually find that what troubles us is that our time has tended to take from us the chance of a fresh start. We seem to have gone back to some ancient period when men seemed to be obsessed by dread fears; when they dared walk only in appointed and carefully charted ways, when they could live and work and talk and deal only with those who are fashioned in their own image, which is to say they could live and work and talk and deal only with people who had precisely the same kind of fears that they had. We seem to have gone back to the age that believed that all things were black or white, when one was either right or wrong, and by fiat, by immutable law, was forever compelled to remain so.

We had every reason to believe until a little time ago that this way of life had become the subject of study for historians and archeologists. We had been told that it was impossible to think in such terms in the crowded, complex world in which we live. Whether he prefers it or not, man must abandon his fears and must believe in his own possibilities; he has to live with his neighbor, however he may be fashioned, and he must accommodate himself to the differences of others, else he cannot survive, and our civilization cannot stand. Our growing needs, and some of them have become so very important to us, call upon the natural gifts and the productive resources of the whole world, our inescapable refinement of functions that men perform, the inevitable specialization of skills and knowledge have forced upon us the necessity to rely upon our neighbors, whether they be near or far. All of this denies us the luxury of permitting the congealing of ideas. It destroys forever any hope that some may cherish of the placid, unchanging, unchallenged way of life in which individuals and whole nations can walk alone in unalterable paths. Simply stated, we can no longer afford inordinate affection or out-of-hand rejection of people or ideas. Our time can no longer tolerate the hard and fast line of thought and action. We cannot be implacable either in our sympathies or in our antipathies. In our relationship with God, we may perhaps yet hold on to certain absolutes; but in our relations with one another, we must deal with open mind and open heart, and for us Americans, for years to come, it appears, with open hand.

Does this have the ring of opportunism? Does it mean that we shall stand firmly at no fixed point? It does not! Our criteria of right, our standards of justice and fairness and truth, our democratic ideals, our goals for man, these must stand— inviolate and uncompromised. But our plans, our platforms, our programs, our contemporary aims, however impelled we are to make them and to announce them, must be resilient and susceptible to change. Now out of this tendency to call all things right or wrong, black or white, we have committed some grievous faults, and of all that, we have perpetrated the most grievous, the one that threatens us most as individuals and a nation, is the spirit of mistrust which hangs as a dark cloud over us whenever we discuss the most relevant issues of life. We call upon one another continually to give proof of loyalty as if every American had been part of the great conspiracy to destroy his country . . . as if one could purge himself of treachery such as this proclaiming his innocence and his loyalty each day. . . . Indeed, we have reached the point of grotesqueness where to have once been a vile traitor and to have confessed and repented, and informed on others, is to be apotheosized, raised to national sainthood; while to have been an honest, earnest, useful citizen with nothing to repent or recant is to render one suspect. We are ready to believe the worst of those who are willing to stand on the sacred documents of American democracy, while we gratefully accept the dimly recollected hearsay evidence of those who are ready to admit that they were ready to destroy these documents altogether. Are there only fifth-amendment Communists? Can there not be also fifth-amendment Americans?

Let me tell you of an incident that was reported by an eyewitness of the utmost probity that reflects the depths of mistrust which we have reached. This incident occurred in Evanston, Illinois, about a month ago when the World Conference of Protestant churches was being held there.

For several weeks during that Conference, we were reading
pronouncements that were made in the press issuing from the
various workshops. Some of them seemed vague when they
talked about Protestant Christian eschatology, about hopes in the
world to come. The more immediate and meaningful expressions spoke of Christian aspirations here on earth. A number
of the proclamations seemed naïve. They dealt with the world
political situation. Among these were some which may have
been communistically inspired. Others had to be made by
individuals who paid these words as a price for leaving the Iron
Curtain lands in which they live, or perhaps more correctly, as
a price for returning to those lands to free their families and
congregations from the role of hostage in which they were
surely held.

During this conclave, a friend of mine, a Christian, who
was attending some of the sessions, observed a cleric wearing
the exotic robes of a church of some Asiatic land. This visitor
in our country stopped to inquire of a local citizen the direction
to his hotel. He was greeted with coarse vulgarity and told by
this champion of democracy, "I would not tell a dirty Communist anything." One can only wonder what happened to
that visitor's faith in the American way of life, or how much
he could take home to his own people, to tell them to emulate
in us. If he was a Communist, and he might have been, how
much was his ideal confirmed; if he loved human freedom, how
much was his ideal shaken. One wonders also what happened
to that American's faith in the American way of life, and what
fears robbed him of his senses. He walks on ground that
Abraham Lincoln walked. He breathed that same air.

It needs to be said that despite naïveté, despite expressions
at that conference that might have been inspired, it would be
grossly unjust, it is grossly unjust to judge as many have, this
great religious profession by these utterances alone. The fact is,
and it is a fact too little brought to our attention, that no country in which Protestant Christians predominate is under the yoke
of totalitarianism. Not one Protestant country is a satellite of
Russia, not one is in a state of crisis on this question which

agitates the world, and it is not because they are geographically or economically, or militarily beyond reach.

While I point out this fact, let another be remembered. The only country in the world in which Judaism is the predominant faith, Israel, has similarly resisted extreme pressures from without and the importunities of a small lunatic fringe from within and has consistently put its weight on the democratic side of the struggle. This point is made for no invidious purpose, but to make clear that we give too much credence and support to an ugly canard when we believe and repeat, what is too frequently said, that Protestants and Jews are soft on this question and do not make effective resistance to communistic atheism. The simple fact is that where these religious professions exercise real influence, communism is at most a vexatious and pestiferous gadfly, and constitutes no Damoclean threat to freedom. This may not always be so, but at this moment, history would have to record the fact in this way.

As all Americans are not guilty of treason or even modified versions thereof, neither are all innocent. A relatively small number of men and women, for reasons that defy explanation, did at one time or another ally themselves with proven enemies of our country in treasonable activities. A large number without the slightest desire of injuring the institutions of American democracy, but with the mistaken notion that they were strengthening them, associated themselves passively with these same proven enemies. A still larger number, in an age of confused values, found intellectual stimulation in this new-old philosophy which seemed to them to offer a solution or an approach to the perplexities of modern life; and they, too, traveled in the company of those who sought to lead the multitude to do evil.

All together—the treacherous, the foolish and the curious—do not constitute a great number. Of all the civilized nations of the world into which this philosophy of naked power and materialism has seeped like a noxious gas, ours has been least affected, both numerically and ideologically. Many books have been written to explain this. The simple reason for our seeming immunity is that we have most to lose by accepting it. And the least favored economically and socially, and the least informed educationally, among us understand this. There is solid truth in the definition of democracy which recognizes that the common ordinary citizen knows what is best for him. And the common ordinary citizen knows it is not totalitarianism in any form. To credit the FBI, however much it deserves our praise, or congressional committees, or a political party, or ambitious politicians with this achievement is to perpetrate a sacrilege against our democratic ideals and our history as a people. In the perpetration of this sacrilege, we have allowed ourselves another throwback to medievalism which tolerated any means for the achievement of a good end. To justify the flagrant violation of human rights, and to tolerate the suspension of constitutional guarantees, in the name of American democracy, makes about as much sense as permanently removing a person's eye because it has a bit of removable dust in it.

These thousands, the treacherous, the foolish and the curious, represent a great danger to us. In small part, small only in the sense that they are few in number, that danger consists in their readiness to betray our country. In greater part, much greater part, we are endangered because their continued separation from us, as lepers who dare not announce their unclean presence, puts every American under a cloud of suspicion. As long as we persist in the idea that having once sinned, grievously or lightly, deliberately or in error, they are forever beyond the pale, just so long will the freedom we prize be curtailed for all of us. Some way must be found for these men and women to examine themselves, renew themselves and be restored so that they may make a fresh start.

More is needed than the newly announced plan of immunity. Perhaps what is wanted is a program of amnesty, a form of absolution, under which those who presently live in danger of public exposure could voluntarily come before authorized officials, indicate the nature of their association, declare their present loyalty, and give as much or as little information as they desire about others associated with them. This amnesty should be offered in good faith and with every possible guarantee of secrecy and immunity from prosecution by the government or persecution by zealots in or out of public office.

The net effect of such a program would bring forth many hundreds of splendid useful citizens who faithfully occupy positions of respect and trust and who dread that someone will remember that they once belonged to a college society, or attended a now proscribed meeting, or made a contribution to a cause which now appears sinister, or read a magazine whose editorial staff contained faithless men, or did any or many things with no intention of being other than good Americans. It will also bring forth some who delved more deeply in this black political art who have broken with it because they discovered its evil ends and violent means. These men and women have learned a bitter and painful lesson and must now live as those who are blackmailed and in dread of exposure. Such an amnesty might even bring forth some who are still deeply caught in the web and cannot leave though they would chose to do so. These might be moved to tell much that is current and useful in the bitter struggle in which our way of life is threatened.

Our holy season has its culmination and climax on the Day of Atonement. The theme of that day is that "God does not seek the life of the sinner, but that he return to Him and live." This should be a guiding principle in all of our human relationships because inherent in it is the belief that there is much worth saving in every human being. Because we need each other so much, because mistrust breeds so rapidly and spoils our chance for a good life with one another, we should pray and work for the time when all people, individually and collectively as nations, will conciliate their differences and find that true reconciliation which will promote peace and prosperity for all the world. Then shall we return again to the way of life which encourages and supports new starts, new hopes, new life for all.

WHEN YOU PRAY, "THY KINGDOM COME," WHAT DO YOU MEAN? [6]

ROBERT J. MCCRACKEN [7]

Dr. Robert J. McCracken preached this sermon at the Riverside Church on Sunday, November 14, 1954. Comparatively unknown when he came from Canada to succeed Harry Emerson Fosdick at the Riverside Church on October 2, 1946, Dr. McCracken early justified the selection by the congregation to this distinguished pulpit. During the past ten years he has continually gained prestige and popularity as a preacher—in his face-to-face addresses to his large Sunday morning congregation, to his radio audiences, and to university and other audiences.

Born in Scotland and educated at Glasgow University, he held pulpits at Edinburgh and Glasgow and became a leader in the Baptist denomination. Later he taught Christian theology and philosophy at McMaster University, Hamilton, Ontario, and became president of the Baptist Convention of Ontario and Quebec, 1945-1946. His preaching ability often led him to address audiences in the United States, especially on topics related to the interests of the Christian church as a whole.

The sermon below illustrates Dr. McCracken's homiletic method: (1) a text is used; (2) the sermon is readily outlined; (3) the illustrations are simple and often drawn from the Bible; (4) Jesus, as leader, is continually made central; (5) the sentence structure is uncomplicated, and the language has little rhetorical embellishment; (6) theological complexities or innovations are avoided. The sermon, in line with Dr. McCracken's concept of ecumenical Christianity, stresses the church and kingdom as concerned with the here and now.

Thy Kingdom come.—Matthew 6:10.

Never a Sunday passes but we gather here and offer that prayer. Millions repeat it every day of their lives. What does it mean? When you use this form of words what is it that you are asking for? Is it a new social order, a world without war or want or fears or tears? Is it an ideal condition of affairs which you associate more with heaven than with earth and do not expect to see realized in history? Is it linked in your mind

[6] Text, with permission for this reprint, furnished through the courtesy of Dr. Robert J. McCracken.

[7] For biographical note, see Appendix.

with an apocalyptic, cataclysmic second coming of Christ? It may be none of these things. Perhaps, repeating the time-worn familiar words by rote, you scarcely give a thought to their meaning or significance.

Jesus was always talking about the Kingdom of God. The phrase occurs in the Gospels over a hundred times. The first sermon He preached had for its text, "The time is fulfilled, and the Kingdom of God is at hand." Parable after parable began with the formula, "The Kingdom of God is like. . . ." All our talk today is about the church and Christianity. He spoke habitually about the Kingdom of God. What did He mean by it? It might be better first to indicate what He did not mean. The term was familiar to His fellow-countrymen. For them it had all sorts of political and nationalistic connotations. It signified independence of Rome and material prosperity.

> They were all looking for a king
> To slay their foes and lift them high.

Here they and Jesus were completely at variance. They emphasized the *Kingdom,* He the *Kingdom of God.* They were thinking of apowerful state that might well become a universal empire; He was thinking, as the Beatitudes show, of a spiritual condition, of qualities like meekness, gentleness and purity and the transformation they could work in human lives and human relationships. "My Kingdom," He said, "is not of this world," meaning it is not material but spiritual, it is not political but moral.

Let us try to grasp more fully what the term involves. The Kingdom of God is the rule of God in the hearts of men and in the life of the world. It is present here and now. Jesus inaugurated it and it owes its reality and power to Him. He does more than point to the prospect of a redeemed society; He calls us to live now as members of God's Kingdom. There have been times when you have done that—on Christmas day when you have lived in the spirit of peace and good will, or when you have freely forgiven an injury or been forgiven, or when some evening you have watched the sun go down like a ball of fire behind the hills and sensed the majesty and glory of

God, or when you said goodbye for the last time to one you loved, and though unspeakably sad at heart, knew that all was well. You may not be able to define the Kingdom of God but you have been in it, even if only for brief, fleeting moments. It is a present reality. Christmas, Good Friday, Easter, Pentecost are the proof of that. Its consummation is still to come but we can have experience of it now. God in His grace and mercy is always entering into these lives of ours.

The Kingdom, Jesus says, is within us. However far it may extend and whatever it may mean ultimately, it begins with the rule of God in our hearts. We are not made members of the Kingdom of God by some accident of birth but by our own voluntary act. Of our own free will we submit our lives to God's rule and seek first the doing of His will. When the scribe said that to love God "with all the heart and with all the understanding and with all the strength, and to love his neighbor as himself, is much more than all burnt offerings and sacrifices," Jesus declared that he was "not far from the Kingdom of God." He understood its secret. Wherever a man or a woman has made Christ the Lord of life and accepted the rule of God in the heart—there is the Kingdom.

Jesus begins with the individual. Why? Because the problem of the social order is basically the problem of human nature. You are not going to solve the social problem until you do something with the individuals who create the problem. As Studdert-Kennedy once said, "To change your government only means taking one lot of sinners out and putting another lot of sinners in." People say that you can't change human nature. But if human nature can't be changed there is no hope of a better world. To talk about changing human nature may sound idealistic, but to talk about changing human society without changing human nature is unrealistic. Men, Jesus kept urging, will never be right with one another until they are first right with God.

This is why He begins with the individual. All renewal and reform start there. "From within outwards," was His fundamental principle. With Him the emphasis was always on personality, and on personality in its spiritual depths, where the secret springs of action are hidden and motives gradually shape themselves. Change men, He said, in their inward nature and you will create the atmosphere out of which social reform will grow. Transform the ideals and purposes of the individual, and the individual so transformed will be eager to make the social order reflect the ideals of the Kingdom.

So the Kingdom, beginning with and in the individual, becomes visible in the world. It starts with single, separate souls but it does not end with them. It goes on to seek the extension of the rule of God in every phase of human life. Its goal is nothing less than a redeemed society, a new moral order. What it stands for is the whole of life acknowledged as belonging to God, His sovereignty recognized in every part of it.

> Thine is the loom, the forge, the mart,
>   The wealth of land and sea,
> The world of science and of art,
>   Revealed and ruled by Thee.
> Then let us prove our heavenly birth
>   In all we do and know,
> And claim the kingdom of the earth
>   For Thee, and not Thy foe.

When you pray "Thy Kingdom come" you are asking that the total life of humanity may be organized with reference to God, home and school, trade and profession, church and state.

Too many persons are individualists in religion. They do not seem to realize that a religion which consists simply or mainly in getting one's own soul saved is something radically different from the faith brought to the world by Christ. It shocked me the other day to come across this sentence from John Henry Newman, author of the hymn, "Lead, Kindly Light." "I have never considered social questions and their relation to the faith, and have always looked upon the poor as objects of pity and compassion." It is useless to sing —

> Jesus shall reign where'er the sun
> Does his successive journeys run;
> His Kingdom spread from shore to shore,
> Till moons shall wax and wane no more—

unless we realize that Jesus must reign in every department of human life, that He is "Lord of the mill as He is of the minster, and as much concerned with the counting house as He is with the cathedral." Financiers, merchants, businessmen, trade union leaders, politicians—they must all bow before Him. The Church is not just a Noah's ark or ambulance cart. It has to do more than rescue a number of individuals out of a lost and ruined world, and bring them to such a pitch of personal piety that they will be guaranteed salvation in the world to come. It is its mission and duty to claim the whole of life for Christ; to enter boldly into the worlds of commerce, industry, education, art, politics, and declare that there as everywhere else His will must be done, and He must be acknowledged as king.

A minister of the Christian church, Alan Richardson, has written a book in which he has really let himself go. I quote one paragraph.

Men do not come to church today because the Christianity of the churches is a sham thing—because of the wide gulf which exists between professed faith and everyday practice. Before men can believe in a Gospel they have to see it lived. The Christianity of the churches is lip-service to a faith which churchgoers do not in fact believe, as is evidenced by their daily lives. There is no radical difference between the lives of churchgoers and non-churchgoers: the former profess to believe in love, the latter do not, but both behave in exactly the same way in the market place. Both are equally concerned with getting and spending; neither is troubled very much about the injustices of society; neither has the remotest idea of what would happen in a community which lived according to the Gospel of God in Jesus Christ.

That faces you and me with a challenge. Are the standards of our lives, in the matter of getting and spending, for example, the standards of the Kingdom? Do we care how other people live? Again and again we pray, "Thy Kingdom come." What are we doing to advance the coming of the Kingdom in our business associations? We are distressed and confused by world problems and their magnitude. There is so little we as individuals can do. Everywhere the reconstruction of society is going on, here by slow change, there by revolutionary upheaval. What is the will of God for us in the matter? It is not easy to say. But what about the tasks that are right at our doors? We are to Christianize all those activities that we are too prone to look on as secular. A Christian businessman should scorn to ask a salesgirl to make untrue statements about goods. He should not buy shares simply because the investment is profitable and irrespective of the character of the operation into which his money goes. Has he a Christian right to accept large dividends without inquiring what the conditions of labor are for the employees? Some time ago the Congregationalists in Britain called to the president's chair a layman, Mr. Angus Watson. Sketching the characteristics of a Christian society from the point of view of an experienced businessman he laid it down that wages should be not merely a first charge on industry but a further charge as soon as the passive owners of capital have received, say 5 per cent, and he quoted arresting examples of the combination of high dividends with, by comparison, scandalously low payments to workers. It was not Mr. Watson's statistics that interested me most; it was the fact that as a businessman he was endeavoring to apply the principles of Christ to business life. For him the Kingdom of God was not just a pious fancy or a Utopian ideal.

What are we doing to advance the Kingdom in the world? It is a Kingdom without frontiers. Its boundaries are coextensive with humanity. In it there is neither bond nor free, male nor female, Jew nor Gentile. All men are alike in fundamental constitution; hence, whatever their nationality or outward condition, all are capable of entrance into the Kingdom. Do we nevertheless, though professing to be Christians, hold out for and maintain distinctions of class and caste, color and nationality? Elton Trueblood provides a concrete example. "A friend of mine," he writes, "was recently in New York City. He went to a great hotel, and, as he stood in line waiting to get a room, there was a colored man, who was very courteous, immediately in front of him. The colored man said, 'I should like a room.' The clerk said, 'No, all the rooms are filled.' The colored man then moved on towards the outside of the lobby. My friend stepped up to the same window and said, 'I should like to have a room.' And the clerk said, 'Yes, what price would you like? You may have it at once.' My friend was the revolutionary kind of Christian. He saw that the colored man wasn't too far away to call him, so he called across the lobby, 'Please come back. This man made a mistake. The rooms aren't all taken because he has just offered me one.' Then he turned to the clerk and said, 'Do you want me to sue you or not? I'm ready to sue you right now.' The clerk answered hastily, 'He can have a room. He can have a room.' " This is Trueblood's comment. "How many of us would have had the courage to do that? Or would we have said, 'That's none of my business'? Unless we can have that kind of religion, that drives into the midst of our lives, that gives us the courage to make a witness in hard situations, the rest of the world isn't going to pay much attention to what we say. But if it could be something as driving as that we could still have a new world."

I have been stressing what we can do to advance the Kingdom of God in the world. Yet let us remember that Jesus said, "It is your Father's good pleasure to give you the Kingdom." First and foremost the Kingdom of God is the gift of God. Don't let us suppose that we can build or establish it ourselves by our concerted efforts. We have a part to play but we can do our part effectively only if we become the channels and instruments of divine power. What God does for men is incalculably more than what men do for God. Our attitude must always be that of waiting upon God, of working with God, of trusting not in our wisdom but in the divine grace and power working in us and through us and accomplishing what we could never do in our own strength. David Grayson tells of an old stonemason who showed him round a village he was visiting. Every now and again the old man would point to some stonework in dyke or cottage and say with great satisfaction, "I was at the building of that"—not *I* built that, but I was at the building of it.

This is the ground of our hope of the *consummation* of the Kingdom. Just as science is built on the assumption that there are certain unalterable laws to which things must conform so our confidence in the ultimate victory of righteousness springs from our faith in God. This was the faith Jesus cherished. This is our faith too. If the hope of the Kingdom's complete realization depended on human initiative or effort we should give up in despair. It does not. Our sufficiency is of God and our hope is in Him. The age-long warfare between good and evil is not going to drag on and on indefinitely or inconclusively. One day it is going to end, and end in a victory for righteousness, in the victory of God. The Christian hope of the realized Kingdom of God brings assurance in our bewilderment and perplexity, renews our flagging energies, provides a goal for our best efforts. The kingdoms of this world will become the Kingdom of our Lord, and of his Christ; and He shall reign for ever and ever.

UNTIL HE COMES [8]

PAUL SCHERER [9]

Dr. Paul Scherer preached this sermon in the Old South Church, Boston, Massachusetts, on November 17, 1955, at the opening service of the National Council of Churches.

One of America's leading present-day preachers of the Lutheran ministry, he has served as pastor of the Holy Trinity Lutheran Church, New York, 1920 to 1945; as radio preacher, Sunday Vespers program, National Broadcasting Company, 1932-1945; and as preacher at various colleges and universities in the United States and England. Since 1945 Dr. Scherer has been professor of homiletics at Union Theological Seminary, New York City. In his teaching he has dealt with preaching methods, sermon construction, expository and doctrinal preaching, sermon composition, and delivery.

The sermon below illustrates the homiletic method of Dr. Scherer's recent years and something of his religious doctrine. He uses a Bible text and saturates his sermon with Biblical quotations and allusions. But he is also given in this sermon to frequent quotations from other sources, such as "a French skeptic," Kierkegaard, "a recent novelist," Nygren, "some pious soul over the air," Jacques Ellul, George MacLeod, Yeats, Winston Churchill, "some wounded soldier."

Dr. Scherer's organization here is better defined than in some of his earlier sermons. His language is unhackneyed, here and there dramatically emotional and imaginative. He is stylistically original. Sometimes the theme of the sermon is repeated in impelling directness: "We are not the elect, handpicked for heaven. We are handpicked for responsibility and peril."

Such statements reveal Dr. Scherer's neo-orthodoxy. Christianity to him calls for participation in the drama of man's sin, sacrifice, and redemption—"the interwrought tragedy and triumph" of the Cross. The church is a sacrificial community. "For that life" [of Christ] she is willing to die, herself in some far off way the suffering servant of mankind." The Kingdom of God is of the here and now ("the time is now"). Its mission is to minister to all, including "the least of these my brethren." [10]

---

[8] Text (slightly abridged) from *The Pulpit.* 27:28-32. January 1956. Permission for this reprint through the courtesy of Dr. Paul Scherer and the Christian Century Foundation, Chicago, Illinois, publishers of *The Pulpit.*

[9] For biographical note, see Appendix.

[10] See also *Representative American Speeches*: 1954-55, G. Bromley Oxnam, "We Intend to Stay Together," p 145-52; Robert L. Calhoun, "Christ—the Hope of the World," p 161-73.

Paul is writing here [I Corinthians 11] of the disorders which have arisen at Corinth in connection with the celebration of the Eucharist, when all at once in the twenty-sixth verse he derives from that central act of Christian worship what is perhaps the most concise and sobering statement you will find in the New Testament of the nature, the mission and the destiny—on this earth at least—of the whole Christian church.

It would seem to me that just here Paul is addressing himself not only to the hopes we cherish for the church of Jesus Christ, but to all the misgivings we have about it, and to everybody who wavers in between the hope and the misgiving without knowing at all what to think of this that we see which God has done, and now he has it on his hands! Said a French skeptic, "Jesus announced the Kingdom of God, but it is the church which has come!" What in the world is it? We have difficulty making it out. What in the world is it for? And what in the world is going to become of it?

I

"You proclaim the Lord's death." It is clear from that what the church is: it is the company of the redeemed, with nothing back of it to keep it from looking foolish but the divine effrontery of a cross! Paul must have done his own wondering about these people at Corinth, and the news he had had of them. It was quite all right that there were "not many . . . wise . . . not many . . . powerful, not many . . . noble." But that was putting it mildly. The trouble was, they were such bumptious fellows besides, know-it-alls and show-offs; and what was still worse, they went about, some of them, with fewer morals than we would have thought decent.

What would you have made of a situation like that? Would you have saluted them as "the church of God which is at Corinth . . . called to be saints"? Would their loud talk and intellectual arrogance have got into your prayer? "I give thanks to God . . . that in every way you were enriched in him with all speech and all knowledge." Would you have seen creation in the midst of that chaos, and felt the winds of God in your face?

Paul did. And he was not just tearing out the silver lining in order to throw the cloud away. It was not *their* faithfulness that would stand its ground, by hook or by crook, by rod or by staff. He knew that. It was *God's,* marching up out of the long past, carrying all its rigors with it: so terrifyingly fixed, as the law of gravity is fixed, that every time you tried to fool with it you proved it! Perhaps that is what foolproof really means. He had unfurled it like a flag at the beginning of his letter: "God is faithful, by whom you were called into the fellowship of his Son, Jesus Christ our Lord." Now he pointed them to the emblem it bore: the emblem of that death which on Calvary had contradicted all their contradictions. "You proclaim the Lord's death." It was in this that he found the challenge of what in fact they *were*; and he set it up in defiance of all they seemed to be. It was in this that he came upon the truest, deepest knowledge he had of them. And it was in this, as nowhere else—in this sign not of a "sacred sorrow" but of a "holy redemption"— that they could know themselves, in the face of life's rebuttals, as the frontier, the very invasion point, of God's history of salvation.

Can we still read the riddle of the church like that? Or must we read it this way? "What we have before us," says Kierkegaard, "is not Christianity, but a prodigious illusion, and the people are not pagans, but live in the blissful conceit that they are Christians. How could it occur to anyone that this is what Jesus Christ talked about?" While to match it, out there in the world, is what one recent novelist has called the "anguished cry of modern man seeking to discover his own identity," and "turning at last for the secret" not to the cathedrals of Europe or the laboratories of the West, but to Africa, where there is still "the smell of the womb"; and when you have found the secret, adds the author, "buried in the jungle," in the "bloody, festering tangle," God knows, maybe it is more than the mind can bear!

Is that it? With nothing any longer to strip the engagement of its ultimate terror? Nothing that can read the terror itself as a footnote? No deep breath among us, for the first time in all the centuries, to breathe, "I thank my God"? This church he has on his hands is the fellowship of his Son, and it is at home in tragedy, even in the very death that haunts its life: it got its start there, where the worst in man met the best in God and said *No* to it unmistakably; only to have him "pound the table hard" with his *Yes,* and set about building the future on it. It is what we are by his deed, not just the body which Christ uses, but *his body,* that we betray yet cannot deny, obscure but cannot destroy. It is still as much a fact about *us* as it is about *him*; pervading human history, "too real," as someone has put it, "to be overlooked," too "vital to be forgotten"; forever taking shape before men's eyes, emerging out of the fog of all our human weakness and blindness and sin, as a family likeness takes shape when the family gathers one by one, or as an image appears on the film as you wash it back and forth under the acid. We may not have what we hope for yonder: by the grace of God we may have more of it here, ashadow of his coming Kingdom, and of what this torn earth could be in his terrible and healing hands.

II

That is what the church is: the fellowship of those whom God in Christ, faithful in our faithlessness, has not only called but redeemed. Then what is it for? "You proclaim the Lord's death." By that same token it is the sacrificial community.

Surely it is significant for us that of all things else in the mind of the apostle, worship, as the characteristic function of that community, should come first. On it the existence of the church depends. To it everything she does about her existence in this world—her organization, her administration, her machinery—is under bond to contribute.

But never can her worship be a means to some end of her own. It is the one means which becomes itself the end. We do not glorify God in order to enjoy him forever, or love him in order to find in that love our own eternal happiness. "Did Luther," asks Nygren, "write two million words for nothing?" Worship itself is the sacrament of meeting, where the conscience is quickened by God's holiness, the mind fed with his truth, the imagination purged by his beauty, the heart opened to his love,

the will devoted to his purpose—not that he is waiting around
to have me accomplish all this as I might whet a knife, but precisely because it is *not* his holiness, or his truth or his beauty,
or his love, or his purpose that he reveals. It is *himself* that he
bestows, in that solemn act of recognition. "Father, I have
sinned!" "My son! My son!"—which issues in the sudden shelter of those arms and the kiss that stops the mouth of my poor
little memorized speech. Our very being here is the soul's Amen
and Hallelujah to that!

Must we ask again, What for? For what other great thing
than the death of our life which is life out of death, and God's
most ancient habit?

Our worship proclaims that. The word Paul uses is exactly
the word he uses for proclaiming the gospel. And to that our
worship commits us. Not alone in the sacrament which she re-
ceives, but in everything that she does, in all her *Gottesdienst,*
her service of his in the world which is his Holy Place, the
church heralds that human life which meant death, because it
was God's life lived down here among men. And by her worship she says that for that life she is willing to die, saving all
she will ever save by spending, finding all she will ever find by
losing, her true greatness not in anything she achieves but only
in what she becomes, herself in some far off way the suffering
servant of mankind.

It may well be in this more than in anything else that we
shall come to realize our oneness. Not by any "loyalty to the
good which is seen to be reasonable." So the president of one
of our colleges has cautiously defined religion. Not by rubbing
out anybody's theology in the name of ecumenicity, or straining
off the question of truth from the question of unity. Not by
adding ourselves to each other in order to get "something of the
same kind, only bigger." But by learning at last to know what
the death is in which the life of God is cradled. Specifically by
that are the rivalries which divide us most bitterly judged: the
members we vie with each other to gather, the preferment we
covet, the pride we take—and we are so sure it is humble pride
—in our separate traditions. "Where she is weak, O God,
strengthen her." But that is somewhere else. It cannot be where

we are. We are one of the few strongholds she has left. "Where she is divided, unite her." But have regard, please, for her officers, and her boards, and her institutions, to make no mention at all of her real estate!

Until we hear the Word of the gospel which speaks of death. It says nothing about God's having to look out for any of us, or for our nation. Maybe that is why it is measurably easier for the World Council than for any National Council to be the symbol of our oneness. Some pious soul over the air the other evening seemed to think that the Almighty was pretty well committed to some sort of protective strategy. "I can't believe," said he, "that the God of all creation, after these tired centuries, would allow men to burn themselves to a cinder." Perhaps he should try a little harder! The Corinthians had put it that way to Paul. Coudn't they count on the covenant grace he had told them about to see them through? And the only answer they got from him was the story of Israel's flight from Egypt: *All* our fathers were under the cloud, and *all* passed through the sea. They did *all* eat the same spiritual meat, and did *all* drink the same spiritual drink. But with *many* of them—it was something of an understatement: only Caleb and Joshua came out alive!— with *many* of them, God, to say the least, was not well pleased: for they were overthrown in the wilderness.

We are not the elect, handpicked for heaven. We are handpicked for responsibility and peril. "As often as you eat this bread and drink the cup." It cannot be understood except as "a call to arms, showing what enemy we have to confront, what warfare we have to wage, what weapons we have to use." "You proclaim the Lord's death." It is a costly word, and it cannot be proclaimed except in the heart of conflict. Writes Jacques Ellul of Bordeaux University, "When we have really seen the plight of our contemporaries, when we know why they will not have anything to do with our 'disembodied' gospel, when we have shared their sufferings, their despair and their desolation, then we shall be able to proclaim it." We are God's shock troops! Christianity never raises as a primary question the defending of this faith or the saving of that institution. It always raises a prior question: Are we caught and held by whatever it is up yonder to which we are bound not just by duty but by the freest choices of our being; not by what we can command, but by what commands us; not by what can carry us through this tragedy of a broken world, but by what can set us about with power to bind up its wounds and bring back into its eyes as we can the light of the knowledge of the glory of God which is in the face of Jesus Christ?

III

But there is one thing more in these words of St. Paul. What is the church? It is the redeemed community. What is it for? It is the sacrificial community, by the very sign and seal of its worship. So what is to become of it? "You proclaim the Lord's death until he comes." It is the community that lives in anticipation of the end. But that is not just a grim kind of mood, with its eyes fixed on another world! It is no—may I use the naughty word?—no eschatological foxhole from which, if you live in Europe, you may look forward, in George Mac-Leod's phrase, to some "celestial concert in thin air" after the last cobalt bomb has exploded, or if you live in the States may expect by foray or strategy safely to force the Lord's hand a little and do his Kingdom gentle violence! Rather is it the knowledge that wherever Christ is, in time or beyond it, there he precipitates the crisis. Wherever he is there is judgment, and there is demand, and there is this present being shaped by that future which is the end without end. It is the knowledge that we have already reached what has been described as our last frontier, and there have encountered not nothingness but God!

It has to do with the judgment under which we stand now. Yeats perhaps got hold of that much when he wrote of the rough beast somewhere in the desert, with its slow thighs, and blank and pitiless gaze, slouching toward Bethlehem to be born. And the culture of which we are a part wants us to see nothing but a Great Ally. "God Bless America!" Did it never occur to you that he may have quite a problem on his hands when he tries to answer that prayer? Worse still, have you never been disturbed by the thought that you might not like his answer? The Jews did not! We used to sing lustily when I was a boy, "Take Jesus with you." No mention was made of where you were going. It did not seem to matter much. Although the sons of Eli lost the ark of God that way, and their lives with it! Winston Churchill was once talking whimsically about our perpetual little panics. "A tiny mouse enters the room," he said, "and all the mighty potentates tremble." Shall God Almighty enter the room and nobody turn a hair? I still remember the sudden chill with which I read of some wounded soldier who looked up at a visitor in the hospital when she said to him, meaning well, "I'm sorry you lost your leg," and answered with a smile, "I didn't lose it, Ma'am; I traded it in for an easy conscience." But an easy conscience is the one thing on earth we can't have—with God around!

Could that be what it means for the church to live in antici-pation of the end? Always this thunder on the left! And could it mean, too, that what is asked of us now has acquired another dimension, and an exigency which we had not dreamed of be-fore, just because the powers of that life to come have already invaded the life that now is? They were all wrong, those early Christians, to mind the clock; but they were nearer right in being wrong, nearer right in their day, counting, than we are with our constant postponements, we for whom the days don't count! "The time is now—" says the radio announcer, and adds some figure from a dial. "The time is now," says the New Testament, and adds nothing but a period. And that means nothing for the way we live but a revolution! It doesn't just enhance our moral idealism, or underscore our Christian principles, or try to make of us impractical perfectionists. It moves in on our morals with the Kingdom of God. It makes clear "what the things are that in the last resort are worth caring about." It casts God's fire on the earth, only to unshackle in the midst of it—his *love!*

And it is his *love* we have got to answer for before the bar of history, if history can ever stop long enough on its way down a steep place to the sea! But never mind that. We have got to answer for it here in the terrible presence of One who never saw anything in heaven or hell but human faces: no golden streets and pearly gates; no flames, except as the refuse burning there in the Valley of Hinnom reminded him of some ultimate horror; only the multitudes on the right hand and on the left. That is what he saw all day long, and nobody among them who knew why he was where he was until he was told. "As you did it . . ." Perhaps the words in my case cannot run without the negative: "As you did it not . . ." And he throws both his arms around people I never paid much attention to: "One of the least of these my brethren."

Is that what these words of Paul mean? "Until he comes." That we have to answer *now* for the love that always supplies what it demands? And more, that this far-off future, all sketched in, right hand and left, around the blessed Lord God and *our* brethren, exists for us as Christians in the present? Is that away there at the end really how it is here, truer of life at this moment than anything else we think of as true, truer than everything else we are willing to submit ourselves to as facts? The one question which is loosed at us, with the sharpest barbs, is whether or not we as Christians can let that future, "As you did it," interpret and determine this present—break into it, control it, fashion it—very much as the curly-headed little Prince Charlie, Elizabeth's son, must let his destiny as England's king shape all the years of his childhood and youth. Or shall we be content instead with what goes by the name of "progress," and turns out to be only the alibi which "a good deal more of the same" has found for itself, as it sneaks in under cover, trying to reconcile us with going on as we are in this hot-rod race where Time presses its foot on the throttle and Death holds itself in readiness to jam on the brakes?

No wonder the apostle writes these same Corinthians later on, in his own impassioned way, beseeching them not to receive the grace of God in vain. To set that inconceivably great thing meager tasks, and reap from it only thin harvests, was unthinkable. Not the grace of God in vain! The depth of his wisdom and the length of his patience, the clarity of his justice and the fullness of his mercy, the gallantry of his love and the steadiness of his power—to harness the tides and turn a flutter mill! Heaven turned wrong side out, its treasure poured on the sand for nothing!

I think our very being here is in answer to his prayer! Even then, and even at best, we are promised no easy victory. Our hopes are not the hope of the world. Christ is. It is his victory, not ours, which "struggles to express itself at every point along the way." Hope is God's word, even if we cannot spell it; and it is his last word, "Until he comes." This death which we proclaim did not transform the world into a place where we can whistle a jaunty tune, as if every story were bound to have our kind of happy ending, and everything at last could be wrapped up in a neat bundle and put away on a tidy shelf. Rather is it a world where tragedy and triumph are so interwrought that we cannot disentangle them: except that in Christ we can see now both the beauty and the terror of life, both the goodness and the severity of God, the fire of his judgment and the solace of his wings, this madness down here held in the splendor of that ultimate love. When the allies landed on the coast of France, Europe was still occupied by enemy troops; but the end was already in the beginning that had been made on the beachheads of Normandy!

"You proclaim the Lord's death until he comes."

APPENDIX

BIOGRAPHICAL NOTES

ALY, BOWER (1903-   ). Born, Crystal City, Missouri; B.S., Southeastern Missouri State Teachers College, 1925; A.M., University of Missouri, 1926; Ph.D., Columbia University, 1941; teacher of English, Southeastern Missouri State Teachers College, 1926-30; successively instructor and assistant professor of English, University of Missouri, 1930-40; successively associate professor and professor of speech, University of Missouri, 1940-   ; visiting professor of speech, Columbia University, summers, 1938, 1941; University of Wisconsin, summer 1939; City College of New York, 1940; University of Hawaii, 1946-47, 1955; member, Speech Association of America (president, 1944); editor, *Quarterly Journal of Speech,* 1951-53; author, *The Rhetoric of Alexander Hamilton,* 1941; (with Wilbur Gilman and Loren Reid) *Fundamentals of Speaking,* 1951.

BENSON, EZRA TAFT (1899-   ). Born, Whitney, Idaho; Utah State Agricultural College, 1918-21; B.S., Brigham Young University, 1926; M.S., Iowa State College, 1927; graduate study, University of California, 1937-38; operated farm, Idaho, 1923-29; in British Isles and Europe, Mission for Church of Jesus Christ of Latter Day Saints, 1921-23; University of Idaho Extension Service, 1930-38; executive secretary, National Council of Farmer Cooperatives, 1939-44; executive officer, American Institute of Cooperation, 1943-53; prominent offices in Church of Jesus Christ of Latter Day Saints; appointed Secretary of Agriculture in the Eisenhower cabinet, January 1953. (See also *Current Biography: 1953.*)

BLAKELY, ROBERT J. (1915-   ). Born, Nebraska; attended Onawa, Iowa, public schools, graduating in 1933; A.B., State University of Iowa, 1937; graduate study in history, Harvard University, 1937-38; editorial writer, Des Moines (Iowa) *Register and Tribune*, 1938-42; Office of War Information, a special assistant to Gardner Cowles, Jr., director of domestic branch of OWI, 1942-43; United States Marine Corps Reserves, 1943-45, commissioned, 1944; forward observer for artillery with the 3rd and 6th Marine Divisions; wounded, Okinawa, discharged as First Lieutenant; with *Register and Tribune*, 1946-48; editorial writer, St. Louis *Star-Times*, 1948-51; with the Fund for Adult Education of the Ford Foundation, May 1951-   ; author of articles in *Foreign Affairs, Travel, Far Eastern Review, American Library Association Bulletin,* and Council on Foreign Relations publications.

DE KIEWIET, CORNELIS WILLEM (1902-   ). Born, Rotterdam, Holland; A.B., University of Witwatersrand (Johannesburg, South Africa), 1923, A.M., 1924; Ph.D., University of London, 1927; student, University of Paris, 1927-28; University of Berlin, 1928-29; LL.D., 1951, New York University Law School; L.H.D., Hobart and William Smith Colleges, 1952; teacher, Southern Rhodesia, 1923-28; successively assistant professor, associate professor, and professor of history, State University of Iowa, 1929-41; professor of modern European history, Cornell University, 1941-51; dean, College of Arts and Sciences, Cornell University, 1945-48; provost, 1948-49, acting president, Cornell University, 1950-51; president, University of Rochester, 1951-   ; naturalized United States citizen, 1939; member, American Historical Society, American Council of Learned Societies (chairman, board of directors), Association American Universities (secretary-treasurer); author, *British Colonial Policy and the South African Republics,* 1929; *Imperial Factor in South Africa,* 1941. (See also *Current Biography: 1953.*)

DODDS, HAROLD WILLIS (1889-   ). Born, Utica, Pennsylvania; A.B., Grove City (Pennsylvania) College, 1909; A.M., Princeton University, 1914; Ph.D., University of Pennsylvania, 1917; LL.D., Grove City, Yale, Dickinson, Rutgers, New York University, Harvard, Williams, Dartmouth, and several other colleges and universities; instructor in economics, Purdue Uni-

League, 1920-28; editor, *National Municipal Review*, 1920-33; professor of politics, Princeton University, 1927-34; president, Princeton University, June 1933-   ; adviser to various foreign governments, including those of Nicaragua and Cuba; trustee, Rockefeller and Carnegie Foundations; member, Phi Beta Kappa; author, *Out of This Nettle, Danger*, 1943, and various articles, surveys, and reports in political science. (See also *Current Biography: 1945.*)

EISENHOWER, DWIGHT D. (1890-   ). Born, Denison, Texas; B.S., United States Military Academy, 1915; Army Tank School, 1921; graduate, War College, 1929; Second Lieutenant, United States Army, 1915; Lieutenant Colonel, Tank Corps, World War I; advanced through grades to General of the Army, December 1944; Chief of Operations Division, Office of Chief of Staff, 1942; Commanding General, European Theatre of Operations, June 1942; Allied Commander in Chief, North Africa, November 1942; Supreme Commander of Allied Land, Sea, and Air Forces in Western Europe, November 1943; Chief of Staff, United States Army, 1945-48; President of Columbia University, 1914-16; assistant professor, political science, Western Reserve University, 1919-20; Secretary of National Municipal versity, 1948-52; appointed Supreme Commander of the North Atlantic Treaty nations, 1950; entered in presidential primaries on Republican ticket, January 1952; elected President of the United States, November 1952; temporarily hospitalized with heart ailment, October 1955; announced willingness to accept renomination for presidency, February 1956; author of *Crusade in Europe*, 1948, *Eisenhower Speaks*, 1948. (See also *Current Biography: 1948.*)

GRUENTHER, ALFRED M. (1899-   ). Born, Platte Center, Nebraska; B.S., United States Military Academy, 1919; graduate, Field Artillery School, 1920; Command and General Staff School, 1937; Army War College, 1939; commissioned Second Lieutenant, Field Artillery, 1918; advanced through grades to Major General, 1943; Chief of Staff, Third Army, 1941-42; deputy Chief of Staff, Allied Force Headquarters, 1942-43; Chief of Staff, 15th Army Group, 1944-45; deputy commander, United States Forces in Austria, 1945; deputy commander, National War College, Washington, 1945-47; director, Joint Staff, Joint Chiefs of Staff, 1947-52; Supreme Commander of the North Atlantic Treaty nations, 1952-56; many decorations, including those of Britain, France, Brazil, Poland, Italy. (See also *Current Biography: 1950.*)

HAND, LEARNED (1872-   ). Born, Albany, New York; A.B., Harvard University, 1893, A.M., 1894; LL.B., Harvard Law School, 1896; LL.D., Columbia University, 1930, and degrees from other representative institutions, including one from the University of the State of New York, 1953; admitted to the bar, 1897; practice of law, Albany and New York City, 1897-1909; United States District Judge, Southern District of New York, 1909-1924; United States Judge, Second District, 1924-   ; contributor to various legal publications; author, *Spirit of Liberty*, 1953. (See also *Current Biography: 1950.*)

HOUGH, LYNN HAROLD (1877-   ). Born, Cadiz, Ohio; A.B., Scio College, 1898; B.D., Drew Theological Seminary, 1905; postgraduate study, New York University; D.D., Mount Union-Scio Colleges, 1912; D.D., Garrett Biblical Institute, 1918; Litt.D., Allegheny College, 1923, University of Detroit, 1928; several other honorary degrees; entered Methodist ministry, 1898; pastor of various churches, 1898-1914, including Crawford (New Jersey), Summerfield Church (Brooklyn); professor of history, Garrett Biblical Institute, 1914-19; president of Northwestern University, 1919-20; professor of homiletics, Drew Seminary and Drew University, 1930-47; member of many important religious and educational organizations, including the Association of Methodist Theological Schools (president, 1942), and executive committee of Federal Council of the Churches of Christ in America; author of many volumes, including *Theology of a Preacher*, 1912; *Man of Power*, 1916; *The Eyes of Faith*, 1920; *Personality and Science*, 1930; *The Church and Civilization*, 1934; *Living Democracy*, 1943; *The Great Humanity*, 1952; preacher in England, 1942, under British Ministry of Information.

McCRACKEN, ROBERT JAMES (1904-   ). Born, Mother-well, Scotland; M.A., Glasgow University, 1925; B.D., 1928; student, Cambridge University, 1937-38; D.D., McMaster University, Ontario, 1946; D.D., Bucknell University, 1947; moved to Canada, 1938; to United States, 1946; pastorates at Edinburgh, Scotland, 1928-31, Glasgow, 1932-37; lecturer, systemic theology, Baptist Theological College of Scotland, 1932-37; department of Christian Theology and Philosophy, McMaster University, Canada, 1938-46; pastor, Riverside Church, New York City, 1946-   ; lecturer in practical theology, Union Theological Seminary, New York City, 1949-50. (See also *Current Biography: 1949.*)

MEANY, GEORGE (1894-   ). Born, New York City; attended elementary and high schools, New York City; journeyman plumber, 1915; business representative, Plumbers Local Union, 1922-34; president, New York State Federation of Labor, 1934-39; secretary-treasurer, American Federation of Labor, 1940-52; elected president American Federation of Labor, November 25, 1952; president, AFL-CIO, December 1955-   . (See also *Current Biography: 1942.*)

NIXON, RICHARD MILHOUS (1913-   ). Born, Yorba Linda, California; A.B., Whittier College, 1934; LL.B., Duke University Law School, 1937; general practice of law, Whittier, California, 1937-43; attorney, Office of Emergency Management, Washington, D.C., 1942; Lieutenant-Commander, United States Navy, 1942-46; member, House of Representatives (Republican, California), 1947-50; Senate, 1951-52; elected Vice President of the United States on the Republican ticket, 1952. (See also *Current Biography: 1948.*)

O'BOYLE, PATRICK A. (1896-   ). Born, Scranton, Pennsylvania; education, St. Thomas College (Scranton), St. Joseph's Seminary (Yonkers), and New York School of Social Work; ordained priest, 1921; curate, St. Columba's Church, New York City, 1921-26; executive director, Catholic Guardian Society; assistant director, Child Care Department, Catholic Charities, New York Archdiocese, 1933-36; executive director, Immaculate Virgin Mission, Staten Island, 1936-43; executive director, National Catholic Welfare Conference, War Relief Services, 1943-47; executive director, Catholic Charities of New York, 1947; Archbishop of Washington, D.C., 1947-   .

PERILMAN, NATHAN (1905-   ). Born, Marietta, Ohio; A.B., University of Pittsburgh, 1926; Hebrew Union College, 1932; graduate study, Columbia University; LL.D., Florida Southern College, 1952; rabbi, Congregation Emmanu-El of New York City, 1932-   ; president, Association of Reform Rabbis of New York City, 1951; member of various other theological committees, including administrative and executive committee, American Jewish Commission, 1945, Anti-Defamation League, 1950; active with National Conference of Christians and Jews, orientation programs in military installations, World War II; member of various honorary societies, including Delta Sigma Rho; contributor, *Universal Jewish Encyclopedia*, 1942; *Reform Judaism*, 1949.

RICHBERG, DONALD RANDALL (1881-   ). Born, Knoxville, Tennessee, July 10, 1881; A.B., University of Chicago, 1901; LL.B., Harvard University, 1904; LL.D., Knox College, 1935; practice of law, Chicago, 1904-33; chief counsel for the railroad unions in government injunction suit, 1922; general counsel, National Conference on Valuation of Railroads, 1923-33; argued National Recovery Act case as special assistant to attorney general, 1935; co-author of Railway Labor Act passed by Congress, 1926, and National Industrial Recovery Act, 1933; general counsel and chairman, National Recovery Administration, 1933-35; member of law firm, Davies, Richberg, and others, Washington, D.C., 1936-   ; executive chairman, National Progressive League, 1932-36; author, *The Shadow Men*, 1911, *A Man of Purpose*, 1922, *Tents of the Mighty*, 1930, *The Rainbow*, 1936, *Government and Business Tomorrow*, 1943, and other publications. (See also *Current Biography: 1949*.)

SCHERER, PAUL EHRMAN (1892-   ). Born, Holly Springs, Pennsylvania; B.A., College of Charleston, South Carolina, 1911, M.A., *magna cum laude*, 1913; B.D., Lutheran Theological Seminary (Mt. Airy, Pennsylvania), 1916; honorary degrees at Roanoke, Charleston, Wittenberg, Gettysburg, and other colleges and universities; pastorates at Holy Trinity Church, Buffalo, New York, 1918-19; Holy Trinity Church, New York, 1920-45; Brown Professor of Homiletics, Union Theological Seminary, New York City, 1946-   ; radio preacher, National Vespers Hour, 1932-45; preacher at various colleges and universities, including Vassar, Harvard, Yale, Columbia; preacher in England, 1930 and 1931; author of *When God Hides, The Place Where Thou Standest, Plight of Freedom,* and other volumes of sermons.

STEVENSON, ADLAI EWING (1900-   ). Born, Los Angeles, California; A.B., Princeton University, 1922; J.D., Northwestern University Law School, 1926; LL.D., Illinois Wesleyan University, Northwestern University, Bradley University; reporter, *Daily Pantagraph* (Bloomington, Illinois), 1924-25; admitted to Illinois bar, 1926; member, Chicago law firms, 1927-41; assistant to Secretary of Navy, 1941-44; chief, Foreign Economic Administration, Italy mission, 1943; assistant to Secretary of State, 1945; adviser, United States delegation, General Assembly of United Nations, London, 1946; United States delegate, General Assembly of United Nations, New York, 1946, 1947; governor of Illinois, 1948-52; Democratic candidate for president, 1952, aspirant for Democratic nomination, 1956; tour around the world, 1953; author of *Speeches,* 1953, *Call to Greatness,* 1954. (See also *Current Biography: 1949.*)

CUMULATED AUTHOR INDEX

An author index to the volumes of *Representative American Speeches* for the years 1937-1938 through 1955-1956. The date preceding the title of each speech indicates the volume in which it appears.

Murrow, E. R. 1940-41, 157-62,
Spring comes to England; 1943-44,
37-45, Orchestrated hell; 1945-46,
33-8, Farewell to England; 1947-48,
200-6, Jan Masaryk; 1951-52, 95-
100, Nominating presidential candidates and democracy; 1954-55,
128-33, Commencement address.

Nelson, D. M. 1941-42, 151-60, Mac-
Arthur day address.
Newton, J. F. 1945-46, 214-22, What
to do with life today.
Niebuhr, Reinhold. 1944-45, 191-4,
The crisis of our time; 1947-48, 227-
34, An adequate faith for the world
crisis.
Nixon, R. M. 1952-53, 72-82, Apolo-
gia; 1954-55, 89-98, Vote Republican; 1955-56, 108-19, The Republican cause in 1956.
Nye, G. P. Jr. 1937-38, 54-60, What
does the European situation mean to
us?; 1938-39, 65-70, For an adequate
defense; 1939-40, 53-60, Neutrality.

O'Boyle, P. A. 1955-56, 151-8, The
vision of faith.
O'Brien, J. A. 1947-48, 235-43, Communism and Christianity.
Oxnam, G. B. 1954-55, 145-52, We
intend to stay together.

Patterson, R. C. 1941-42, 135-41, The
sixth column.
Peale, N. V. 1954-55, 153-60, How
to have good relations with other
people.
Pepper, C. D. 1940-41, 49-56, All-out
aid to Britain; 1946-47, 67-88,
Against aid to Greece and Turkey.
Perilman, N. A. 1955-56, 159-66,
Making a new start.
Peterson, H. C. 1939-40, 191-207,
Propaganda.
Phelps, W. L. 1939-40, 364-74, Ac-
ceptance of American Education
award.
Phillips, H. C. 1950-51, 161-8, Re-
ligion—a prop for the weak?
Powell, A. C. Jr. 1949-50, 154-8, For
the Federal Fair Employment Prac-
tices act.
Prentis, H. W. Jr. 1941-42, 201-17,
Preserving the roots of liberty; 1944-
45, 217-28, Competitive enterprise
versus planned economy.
Price, Byron. 1946-47, 213-21, We
must recapture valor.
Pusey, N. M. 1953-54, 193-201, A
religion for now.

Rahskopf, H. G. 1950-51, 141-9,
Speech at mid-century.
Randall, C. B. 1951-52, 112-23, Explaining what, to whom; 1954-55,
55-69, Our foreign economic policy.
Rayburn, Samuel. 1948-49, 155-64,
Repeal of the Taft-Hartley law. A
debate.
Redfield, Robert. 1944-45, 197-9, The
crisis of our time. A discussion.
Reuther, W. P. 1945-46, 165-79,
Should industry grant labor's de-
mands for a 30 per cent wage in-
crease? A debate; 1947-48, 103-17,
The American standard of living:
how can it best be improved? A
discussion; 1949-50, 189-95, United
Automobile Workers: aims and programs; 1951-52, 123-8, Labor's prin-
ciples and program.
Reynolds, Quentin. 1944-45, 123-33,
The campaign and men in uniform.
Reynolds, Robert. 1939-40, 86-116,
America's policy toward insular pos-
sessions of other countries. A sym-
posium.
Rice, G. P. Jr. 1949-50, 220-9, The
scholar in the twentieth century.
Richberg, D. R. 1955-56, 67-77, How
shall we deal with labor union
monopolies?
Robinson, E. E. 1942-43, 221-33, Can
democracy survive the war?
Rockefeller, J. D. 1944-45, 291-7, The
Christian church—what of its future?
Romney, G. P. 1945-46, 165-79,
Should industry grant labor's demands for a 30 per cent wage increase? A debate.
Roosevelt, E. A. 1939-40, 173-82,
Civil liberties—the individual and
the community.
Roosevelt, F. D. 1937-38, 11-16, Second inaugural address; 1937-38, 101-
10, Victory dinner address; 1938-39,
25-8, Canadian position of the
United States; 1938-39, 36-9, United
States policy toward war; 1938-39,
97-107, New Deal must continue;
1939-40, 21-5, This nation will remain neutral; 1939-40, 26-37, Message to Congress; 1939-40, 76-83,
Italy enters the war; 1939-40, 117-
25, National defense; 1940-41, 19-
32, Preservation of American independence; 1940-41, 57-74, A state of
emergency exists; 1940-41, 125-36,
Republican leadership and national
defense; 1940-41, 185-6, Four human
freedoms; 1941-42, 15-18, War address; 1941-42, 30-9, America accepts the challenge; 1941-42, 247-50,
Eight common principles for a better
world; 1942-43, 15-29, Message to
Congress; 1942-43, 217-20, Trusts

15707

1570

THIS BOOK MAY BE KEPT